THE BEST IDEA IN THE WORLD

HOW PUTTING RELATIONSHIPS FIRST TRANSFORMS EVERYTHING

THE BEST IDEA IN THE WORLD

HOW PUTTING RELATIONSHIPS FIRST TRANSFORMS EVERYTHING

FOREWORD BY
MICHAEL SCHLUTER

MARK GREENE

ZONDERVAN®

ZONDERVAN.com/
AUTHORTRACKER
follow your favorite authors

ZONDERVAN

The Best Idea in the World
Copyright © 2009 by Mark Greene

Requests for information should be addressed to:

Zondervan, *Grand Rapids, Michigan* 49530

Library of Congress Cataloging-in-Publication Data

Greene, Mark, 1955 –
    The best idea in the world : how putting relationships first transforms
  everything / Mark Greene ; and a foreword from Michael Schluter.
        p.   cm.
    Includes bibliographical references.
    ISBN 978-0-310-29075-9 (softcover)
    1. Love — Religious aspects — Christianity. 2. Interpersonal relations —
  Religious aspects — Christianity. 3. Friendship — Religious aspects —
  Christianity. I. Title.
  BV4639.G745   2009
  241'.677 — dc22   2009026958

All Scripture quotations, unless otherwise indicated, are taken from the *Holy Bible,
New International Version*®. NIV®. Copyright © 1973, 1978, 1984 by International
Bible Society. Used by permission of Zondervan. All rights reserved.

Interior design by Michelle Espinoza.

Printed in the United States of America

09 10 11 12 13 14 15 • 21 20 19 18 17 16 15 14 13 12 11 10 9 8 7 6 5 4 3 2 1

For the Trinamic Trio,
Anna-Marie, Tomi and Matt,
Knights of the Oblong Table, SPLY.

CONTENTS

A Pause for Gratitude   9
Looking for the Big Idea   11

1 The Big Question   15
   Or *What a Difference a Lens Makes*

2 The Disconnected Heart   27
   Or *Hard Times in the Hard Rock Café*

3 Reconnecting the Arteries   39
   Or *How to Buy a Microwave*

4 Getting Relational Thinking to Work   47
   Or *The Power of Chocolate*

5 Two's Company, Three's a Party   73
   Or *A Tale in Two Parts*

6 The Long Good Love Story   85
   Or *Making the Desert Bloom*

7 Intimacy and the Divine   105
   Or *Tales of Fish and Liver*

8 Loving without God?   123
   Or *What the Atheist Discovered*

9 The Relational Community   137
   Or *The Challenge to the Church*

10 Got a Better Idea?   149
   Or *Give This One a Try*

Notes   153
Taking Relational Living Further   156

A PAUSE FOR GRATITUDE

This little offering is about a simple but very big idea. As it happens, it's not my idea. And it's not the idea of the person who helped me begin to understand it for the first time. Still, without that person's ability to focus my lenses, I would perhaps never have seen it. And so, for Michael Schluter and the book called *The R Factor* that he wrote with David Lee, I am truly grateful. For years I tried to cajole Michael into writing a short version but, though he may have the mind of an Erasmus, he has the stubbornness of a cliff and consistently demurred. In the end, he asked me to write it. Then he started cajoling me.

Many others have helped along the way, not least my colleagues at LICC (London Institute for Contemporary Christianity). In particular, I owe a great deal to Christina Winn, whose combination of perspicacity and personal engagement have been invaluable; to Stephanie Heald, whose selfless, thoughtful brilliance added yeast to the whole loaf; to Helen Valler, whose antennae for clarity are highly tuned; and to team Zondervan – Dudley Delffs, Bob Hudson and Jane Haradine – whose every suggestion made it better.

Originally, of course, the understanding of the vital significance of this idea comes from the mind of Jesus, though, as experience has shown, you don't have to be one of his followers to reap some of its benefits, even if you will miss out on the greatest harvest. Despite its elegant brilliance, however, there is much more to the wisdom of Jesus than this big idea. Nevertheless, there are few that offer such a simple, rich, practical and integrated way forward in every aspect of life – Monday to Monday.

I hope you will be as grateful for it as I am.

Mark Greene
The London Institute for Contemporary Christianity
September 2009

LOOKING FOR THE BIG IDEA

I first started wondering about whether money really made the world go round when working in Africa as an economist thirty years ago. The World Bank, for whom I was working at the time, had plenty of capital to throw at the problems of poverty and ethnic tensions. But money clearly was not providing solutions to the underlying malaise. The free market has no solutions to the problems of political competition and embedded ethnic distrust.

So where could I seek an answer?

Coming out of a Christian background, I turned to its ancient Scriptures. I was in for some surprises. Hard work, thrift and risk-taking are certainly commended, and biblical laws also require regular debt release, community government and strong family life. However, my main difficulty was that I couldn't find the "big idea". What held all these laws together? What is at the heart of the Bible's approach to economic and social justice and to political as well as personal peace?

Then, in plain view in the pages of the New Testament,

but partially concealed by overfamiliarity, I noticed how Christ points not only to a new way of thinking about the big issues of politics and economics but also to a new way of living day to day in the small things of life that so often determine our happiness. The key to this new way of thinking and living is a fresh understanding of both love for God and love for neighbour. And love, of course, is an expression of relationship.

This focus on relationships applies to both public life and private life. As far as my personal experience is concerned, I can say that it has gradually transformed my life. As my wife will readily testify, the process has been extremely slow and still has a long way to go. Indeed, the irony is that the more conscious I become of the "relational dimension" of every aspect of my life, the more unrelational I realise I am in what I think, do and say. Perhaps it is inevitable that as a person draws closer to a relational God, they become ever more aware of their failure to understand and practise the kind of relationships that a perfect God calls for.

For a long time I have wanted to communicate to the Christian public and beyond the riches of this new way of thinking. But I know my gift does not lie in writing readable prose. The answer, I thought, must be to delegate the task. My friend Mark Greene was my first choice, as he has demonstrated repeatedly his ability to understand where most Christians are coming from, and he walks the talk. He eventually gave way to my persistent nagging. Good things come to those who wait. I am immensely grateful to him for making the time both to reflect on and articulate the message.

From whatever religious or ideological starting point you are coming, may I commend to you *The Best Idea in the World*.

Michael Schluter, CBE
Jubilee Centre
Cambridge
September 2009

Still, the memory shimmers
in the depth of our souls,
the memory of how close,
how close we all once were.

Chapter 1

THE BIG QUESTION

OR
WHAT A DIFFERENCE A LENS MAKES

I was twenty-three at the time, young and eager in my first suit, working in advertising, with a spring in my step and a flower in my buttonhole. It was 1978 and wearing a flower in a buttonhole, except for weddings, had ceased to be any kind of a convention at least 150 years before. Still, I rather liked it, and it distracted attention from the fact that I only had two suits and no more than three ties.

Michael Baulk was already a legend in the agency, slim and crisp in beautifully tailored beige suits, driving a sleek Ferrari and inspiring confidence in clients, hard work in subordinates and a good measure of awe from us new trainees. It was an awe only mildly tempered by our sense that, for some of our more senior colleagues, this man's determination and focus seemed a little too intense, a little too steely, merciless perhaps, to trust him with the agency's heart. Nevertheless, we knew that to be chosen to work for him would be like being recruited for MI6 – he emanated excellence.

Anyway, about three months into the job, we trainees were clucking away in a cubicle at the end of the day and "he" appeared, still crisp and perfectly groomed in his beige and unrumpled suit, the creases of his trousers sharper than a surgeon's scalpel. And there in the disarray of that dark and tiny cubicle, far from the bright lights and wide-open spaces of his office, he began to talk about advertising, about what it would take to succeed in this business and about the need for mentors to help us along the way. I was transfixed. It was as if the pope had paused by my shed and was pouring out his wisdom. Who were we to merit such attention? Then Michael said this: "The key to great advertising is strategic relevance and creative brilliance." There it was in a nutshell.

We'd been to countless seminars, read piles of documents, talked to lots of people, been in every department in the agency, but here it was, five words that cut through to the very heart of the matter: "Strategic relevance and creative brilliance" – make sure you are saying the right thing, and then say it brilliantly. Of course, that doesn't make creating great advertising any easier. Strategic relevance takes hard work to fashion, and creative brilliance can't be conjured by just adding an egg. Still, it immediately gave us two simple criteria to judge any work we did.

If only life were that simple.

Perhaps it can be. Imagine someone asked you, "What is the key to the good life?"

How would you reply? <u>What is the one thing you would want to pass on to someone that would help them lead a fulfilling life?</u>

Of course, the ideal answer would have to answer the big questions, like the pursuit of happiness, the ideal partner and the perfect cappuccino, and it would have to give us simple criteria for answering all the little questions we face every day – where to live, what to eat, what to drink, what to buy, how to travel, how to use our time well, how to choose a job …

We need a "lens" that not only helps bring the big picture into focus but also helps us see all the little things in their right perspective. We need bifocals.

This book is about one man's answer to that question, an answer that is like that wonderful moment at an optician's when, having already popped a variety of lenses into the machine, they slide in the last one – and you can tell a "u" from a "v" and an "e" from a "c" – from 100 yards.

There's the story, a true story as it happens, of a teacher of the law asking a popular but unorthodox rabbi this question: "What is the most important commandment of all?"

That rabbi's reply is the key to the good life, the key to a better society and the key to the restored heart – the best idea in the world.

Of course, in an age of media hype and advertising huff and puff, it's hard for us to take claims about the best or the greatest too seriously. After all, we've had endless lists ranking the best and the worst of everything – from films to futons, from the rich list to the hitch list, from goal of the season to blouse of the year, from the top 100 best ads to the top 100 places to eat sushi in Sydney. Still, for many a man and woman in first-century Israel, the question, "What's the most important commandment of all?" was of great significance. Nor was the man who came to ask the rabbi Jesus that question the only person recorded posing it. Clearly, it was an important question.

And it wasn't necessarily an easy question to answer. After all, back in the first century AD, there were rather a lot of commandments for a devout Jew to choose from. Not just the Big Ten but some 613 that the rabbis had identified. It's one thing to look for a needle in a haystack. At least the needle is qualitatively different from straw and you can always use a magnet, but choosing one from among 613 divinely ordained commandments is more akin to trying to pick out the best pearl from a bucket of perfect pearls.

Nevertheless, despite having more commandments to choose from than types of yoghurt in a San Diego supermarket, Jesus, the rabbi, replies with an answer that is swift, simple and succinct, unembellished by parable or delayed by questions of his own:

> "Love the Lord your God with all your heart and with all your soul and with all your mind and with all your strength." The second is this: "Love your neighbour as yourself."
>
> Mark 12:30 – 31

Jesus' answer doesn't come as a surprise to the teacher of the law, but though the man agrees with Jesus, he perhaps doesn't see the extraordinary implications of what Jesus is saying. "Oh, yes," the man might have thought, "we know that. You're right. But there's nothing so desperately radical about that. I know God is to be loved with all that I am and all that I have. And I know that I am to love my neighbour. Life can perhaps go on as usual."

Obviously, there are atheists who wouldn't agree with the command to love God. And there are people of a variety of faiths who would correctly point out that the character and purposes of the God of Jesus are in reality very different from the character and purposes of the Allah of Muhammad or the deities of the Upanishads – all roads do not lead to Rome. Still, not many people take serious issue with the call to "love your neighbour as yourself" even if they might actually go about loving their neighbours in somewhat different ways.

However, it is one thing to know something and quite another to work out the implications of an idea so familiar, so perhaps taken for granted, that it no longer has much force in reality, no longer really shapes the way we live our lives.

In fact, Jesus' response is perhaps even more radically countercultural today than it was 2,000 years ago.

To a culture trying to push God to the periphery, Jesus says, "Put God in the centre." Because human beings are spiritual beings.

To a culture obsessed with rights and the dead-end trinity of me, myself and I, Jesus says, "Focus on others."

To a culture suffering from epidemic levels of loneliness, depression and alienation, Jesus says, "Focus on community."

To a culture obsessed with acquiring quality things, Jesus says, "Focus on building quality relationships."

Indeed, the simplicity of Jesus' answer should not distract us from its significance. If this is the most important commandment, then it reflects what is most important to God. What, then, is most important to God? How we love. How we love him and how we love our neighbour.

And love is fundamentally about relationship. So the thing that is most important to God is:

1a. The quality of our relationships with him.
1b. The quality of our relationships with others.

Christianity is not a "system" to be followed, a body of rules to obey, hurdles to jump or boxes to tick, but a particular kind of friendship with God and people. Of course, at first glance, this focus on relationship sounds all rather fluffy and vague, but, as we shall see, the call to love is not a call to sit around meditating on eternal truths in a blissful reverie but rather a summons to become involved in a down-to-earth movement to make the world a better place. Romantic love may begin with a walk in the park, but it ends up with a discussion about who's going to pick up the kids from school this afternoon. True love is not just about drowning in the intoxicating gaze of the beloved, but about making decisions, doing things for our beloved that makes their life better. Indeed, if you love someone, you think about the impact on them of everything you do and say.

So then, against God's most important criteria, how am I doing?

How is my relationship, my adventure with God? Even the question brings me up short. How is it really? Dynamic or distant? Excited or indifferent?

How is my family doing?

Do we relate well? Yes, we love each other, we're family. But are we like the Finns who, when asked whether the Russians are their friends or their brothers, tend to reply: "Our brothers. Because you can choose your friends." Is there anything truly dynamic, purposeful or enriching about the way we relate? Sometimes I wonder whether I am really helping my kids grow as people or am I just servicing their food, financial and transport requirements. How easy to let mealtimes become mere pit stops between school and homework. How easy for me to let the sheer number of times I have to drive my teenagers to *their* fun activities turn into a chore rather than a great opportunity to chat, chill, listen to music they like and try to like it too, and sometimes find out what's really going on in their lives.

And what about my relationships at work? After all, apart from some romantic liaison, the very idea of "love" in the workplace sounds like an alien concept. But if my relationships with the people I spend so much time with are not characterised by any genuine, benevolent interest, what does that say about me? Am I just there to share the carpet, collect my paycheck and one day maybe attend their funerals, only to realise that I knew nothing much about them except that they liked to leave their tea bag in their cup 'til the water was the colour of coal but then still add lots of milk?

And if I am a churchgoer, what is the quality of relationships there? Yes, we know we're meant to love one another. But what does that mean exactly? Is there more to it than polite affability? Safe, social but superficial.

I wonder, when you think of the quality of your own

relationships and the quality of relationships in your town or your nation, what word or thought pops first into your mind?

Loving?

No road is long with good company.

Turkish Proverb

Q: All the lonely people,
where do they all come from?

Lennon, McCartney

A: Down your street.

Chapter 2

THE DISCONNECTED HEART

OR
HARD TIMES IN
THE HARD ROCK CAFÉ

We were twenty-two at the time and we'd been going out for nearly three years, almost the entire time we'd been at university. We'd seen each other almost every day, and, in that period, we'd probably spent more time together than most married couples. We'd broken up by mutual consent, rightly I knew, but with all the difficulty and, for me at least, the agony that comes from trying to extricate the long roots of one heart from the roots of another. In the end, it took me six years. I will always be grateful. But it took me six years.

Indeed, quite soon after our parting, I wanted her back. Quite desperately really. She was going out with someone else, but, I suppose, the sheer desperation of my heart, of my letters, my calls softened her towards me. We met in central London for lunch. I think she regretted coming. For some reason, we chose to go to the Hard Rock Café. Maybe because it was convenient. Or maybe because it was the only place we could think of, or maybe because it was relatively new in those days and still had a certain patina of cool.

But it was the wrong place. Not the food but the environment with its pulsing, confident, the world-is-my-oyster feel. And it wasn't named the Hard Rock Café because of the texture of its cakes. The music was loud, even for a twenty-two-year-old. You had to nearly shout to make yourself heard, perfect for a frisky flock of twenty-somethings fizzing with good cheer and out for a fine time, but it was wrong, devastatingly wrong, for a confused, bruised Romeo trying to find a way to reconnect the delicate arteries of two hearts. It couldn't be done in that environment. It wouldn't have mattered if I'd had the eloquence of Shakespeare. You can't recite a sonnet in a disco and expect a princess to melt. In the end, of course, the choice of venue wasn't that important – we weren't right for each other.

Still, the reality is that it takes more than good relational skills to develop and nurture the kind of friendships and communities we yearn for. We also need the ability to manage and change our cultural environment. The context around us either makes it easier to connect – or more difficult. Sadly, the soil and climate of Western culture is aggressively hostile to the kind of good life we yearn for. Our habitat is being degraded, and one of the biggest casualties is the quality of our relationships.

Indeed, in the US, the UK and Australia, the quality of our emotional life, our relational life and our community life has rarely been poorer. All the research suggests that we are less happy than we were a generation ago. The recent wave of "happiness" studies is enough to bring tears to a Tigger. In the UK, for example, we have never been so depressed, or at least we have never taken so many antidepressants – prescriptions doubled from 12 million in 1991 to 24 million in 2001 and rose to 31 million in 2006.[1] Our divorce rate is the third highest in the European Union, membership of clubs has declined and involvement in community activities has plummeted. Plenty of kids want to become Cubs and Brownies, but the Brown Owls who lead them are becoming rarer than penguins in the Sahara.[2]

As the 2007 UNICEF report made clear, British children are the most unhappy, neglected and poorly educated in the developed world, ranking twenty-first of the twenty-one countries surveyed. Children in the US are twentieth. And British children rank at the bottom in terms of happiness; abuse of sex, drugs and alcohol; and at the bottom in terms of family and friends. Indeed, British children were found to have the worst relationships in the developed world.[3] Even if you dispute the research, even if somehow the UK managed to claw up the rankings a bit, you only have to talk to the police or to doctors or to teachers to know that we are rearing an increasingly anxious, disaffected, self-oriented generation. The picture is virtually identical in the US.

Of course, *everyone* knows relationships are important, but if it's so obvious, why is it that so much of the way we live life today has served to undermine the quality of our relationships?

In the West we are suffering from an epidemic of loneliness. As anthropologist Margaret Mead put it: "One of the oldest human needs is having someone to wonder where you are when you don't come home at night." [4] The number of people who don't have such a "someone" is soaring. In the UK, single-person households have risen from 18 percent in 1971 to 39 percent in 2007.[5] We may know more people, but we have fewer friends and we spend less time with the people we say are important to us than thirty, forty or fifty years ago.

Yet we hardly realise how lonely we are. We stumble upon that sinking realisation only when we think about throwing a party and have so few people we really know to invite. Or we move to a new job or lose our job and realise that the relationships we had at work, however agreeable, never created a bond that would survive the loss of daily contact and shared tasks. Indeed, recently I realised that some of the people I consider to be my really good friends are people I actually see only once or twice a year. How on earth did this happen?

We have a myriad of ways to communicate with people (and their avatars) – mobiles, texts, emails, webcams, instant messaging, blogs, Twitter, MySpace, Facebook, Bebo, Second Life – and yet we feel out of touch, disconnected from the kinds of relationships that thrill our souls and give our spirits wings. We are globally wired but relationally disconnected, touched a million times a day but rarely embraced.

Not surprisingly, perhaps, we also trust other people much less. And this has had a significant effect on the quality of our working lives. Indeed, even before the credit crunch, there was a crisis of trust in English-speaking Western societies that deeply affected the profitability and effectiveness of almost all our institutions and businesses. One of the keys to sustainable profitability for a business, according to research, is the extent to which people trust their managers. Low trust, low motivation. High trust, high motivation. High motivation, higher performance. Indeed, Gallup surveys have shown that one of the three most important indicators of job satisfaction is whether someone in the organisation actually cares about the employee as a person.[6] Seventy percent of people don't leave their jobs, they leave their managers.[7] And high turnover costs money in recruitment, in training, in lost productivity. Relationships really, really matter to the bottom line.

This decline in trust has had a similar impact on investment. After all, if you don't trust the numbers on the balance sheet, you won't invest in a company, and if companies are starved of investment, they are unlikely to grow. Sadly, the financial crises of 2008 and 2009 only served to accelerate a trend that was already there. Now, it seems, we can't even trust those sombre bankers in conservative suits to do the right thing. And if you can't trust the banks, who are you going to trust? Overall, trust has been melting faster than the polar ice cap. All this helps to explain the tremendous electoral appeal of Barack Obama – people in the US were yearning for a president they felt they could trust.

Thinking about the impact of decisions on relationships matters at work and it matters in politics too. Fundamentally, the primary role of politicians should be to help create conditions in which people can flourish as whole human beings in an ordered, benevolent society. However, in the US and the UK, the overall thrust of government policy has actually created conditions that have made us unhappier than other "developed" nations. We have pursued a form of capitalism that is much more concerned with economic growth than it is with the social impact. By contrast, continental European capitalism is much more relational. For example, successive French governments have been prepared to accept lower rates of economic growth to preserve the quality of community life.

Indeed, in our society, the last twenty years have seen the introduction of a myriad of social policies and trends that have combined to undermine the quality of relationships. We've seen urbanisation and suburbanisation, school relocations outside neighborhoods, the closing of local hospitals, a decline of "live" entertainment venues, a rise in single-parent families, a rise in two-parent working families, all of which, if nothing else, means that adults spend less time with their children.

Space forbids expanding on these, but consider, for example, how ever-increasing commuting distances mean that we're away from our homes for a greater proportion of the day and have less time not only for friends and family but also for community activity.

Our isolation has also been increased by the introduction of a host of new technologies – many wondrous in themselves – but which nevertheless reduce the amount of time we spend building friendships. In the US the average household now has more TV sets than people.[8] This individualisation of leisure is being reinforced by the two PC, one DVD, one PlayStation, two iPod household, which is, of course, incomplete without a car with a built-in DVD to prevent the psychological trauma of long and winding journeys playing "I spy" and singing along to songs on the radio or, heaven forfend, actually talking to the aging "chauffeur" in the front. Increasingly, individual members of families are locked away in their own worlds – real or virtual – and the number of things they do together has plummeted. Of course, there's nothing intrinsically wrong with these technologies but, in most cases, the more there are of "them", the fewer there are of "us". Most people would rather talk to friends than watch TV, but most people spend more time watching TV than talking to friends. We are losing the art of conversation.

Of course, deep relationships have never been that easy to develop, and I'm certainly not suggesting that there was some golden age of relational paradise. Still, the way that Western society currently operates makes rich relationships much harder to develop and maintain, quite independent of any of the personal challenges most of us face in nurturing the relationships we'd like. In the West, we're in a desert. Sure, things grow, but there are a lot of spikes around.

Is the reason for this that we don't think relationships are important?

In some businesses and institutions the quality of relationships is essentially ignored. After all, what do relationships have to do with maximising productivity, profitability and shareholder value? Actually, as it turns out, a great deal. Similarly, in our private lives, though most of us know that relationships are important, we find it hard to live that way. In a culture that vaunts the individual and has done so much to erode community, we have not developed the tools to help us predict the likely impact of our decisions on our relationships. We buy our kids a TV for their bedroom and then wonder why they never seem to be around.

Yet our thirst for intimacy continues undiminished and unsatisfied. Cut off from any vibrant connection to the divine, and increasingly impotent to form relationships of intimacy, Western culture has given its thirsty heart to the obsessive acquisition of things and the anxious, approval-seeking display of logos. I display therefore I am. *Logo ergo sum.*

Psychologically, this seems like a regression to an infantile stage. When mothers begin to wean infants from the breast, the infants are often given an object – a blanket, a teddy bear, a wooden spoon – that becomes a comfort to them, a substitute for the close relationship they enjoyed with their mothers. And this object often accompanies them for months, even years. The object becomes a surrogate, a temporary substitute for the relationship they yearn for.

Most children grow out of this.

Western culture has not. We try to substitute objects for relationships.

These then are the conditions of Western life. Busy, busy, busy, distracted, flitting, with the attention span of a proton in a particle accelerator. And it has left us lonelier than we've ever been.

Jesus' response to the teacher's question – which is the most important commandment? – directly addresses these issues, the personal, the cultural and the political. In the following chapters, we will look at some tools to help us apply Jesus' focus on relationships to everyday life and we'll explore something of what he actually meant by "love" – a word so devalued in our culture that it is almost bereft of meaningful content.

Jesus' No. 1 principle, however, isn't just a helpful piece of wisdom that might make your life a bit better or your business more profitable. Jesus' response reflects the very essence not only of his teaching but of the nature of God – life, and indeed Christianity, is meant to be lived in meaningful relationships. As such, relationships are not an optional extra to the good life, they are utterly essential. Jesus' response has huge implications for society as a whole, for local communities, and, indeed, for every human being. In sum, Jesus' simple response – love God, love your neighbour – reflects the heart of the heart of all that really matters.

Either friendship or death.

The Talmud

*The quickest way to destroy a
personality is to isolate it.*

Lady Diana, Princess of Wales

*The Government will admit anything
other than that its social policies, and those
of previous governments, over the past 40
years have fashioned a psychopathic society
in which an uncomfortably large part of the
population looks on other people in a purely
instrumental fashion, as means for the pro-
curement of their immediate ends. It feels
no social bond with them whatsoever.*

Theodore Dalrymple, *The Times*, 2007

Chapter 3

RECONNECTING THE ARTERIES

OR

HOW TO BUY A MICROWAVE

If relationship is so important, what happens when you start to evaluate your decisions in terms of their impact on relationships?

Take something simple like buying a microwave. What criteria might we use to decide whether or not to buy a microwave?

Well, at first glance, such a decision doesn't look as if it would affect your relationship with God – though perhaps the purchase might possibly put you in debt. Or perhaps there's something else he might want you to do with the money – give it to a charity or buy an easel and paints for a friend. But how about how it might affect your relationships with people?

Imagine this:

It's 3.42 a.m.

Pitch black outside. Chilly inside. In the dim distance down the corridor, beyond two half-closed doors, the snuffling begins to rise to a whimper ... It's going to happen and it's my turn.

The whimper will grow to a cry, to a wail, to an insistent howling crescendo that will make an air-raid siren seem as unintrusive as a hamster bell ... It's going to happen. And it's my turn. Blearily I swivel myself out of bed, gathering momentum like a fighter pilot scrambled ... and scoot downstairs, flicking the kitchen light on as I slide toward the fridge ... fifteen seconds and counting. The bottle is already in there. I grab it, stand it in the waiting pan of water, turn on the gas and wait ... one minute, two minutes ... Upstairs the cry has turned into a wail ... I try the milk. Duh. Too hot. I scurry to the fridge, transfer some from another bottle ... Upstairs the wail has turned into a howl. And everyone in the house, and indeed within a forty-mile radius, has woken up – grim, growling and grumpy.

If I'd only had a microwave.

Imagine:

I hear the whimper. It's going to happen. And it's my turn. Blearily I swivel myself out of bed, gathering momentum like a fighter pilot scrambled ... and scoot downstairs, flicking the kitchen light on as I slide toward the fridge ... 15 seconds and counting ... take two paces to the right, punch the button and the glass door swings out ... 19 seconds. I catch it in my left hand and place the bottle on the glass plate with my right ... 21.5 seconds. Push the door gently to ... 23 seconds. And press the one-minute pad. Forty seconds later, I press the button and grab the warmed bottle, swivel and dash for the door, flicking the light off as I exit and turn up the stairs, shaking the bottle as I go to ensure that the milk is evenly heated. I can hear the whimpering. Eight seconds later I'm in the room ... 2 seconds later the bottle is in the mouth ...

Total: 73 seconds.

Not bad. And good enough. The whimpering subsides; crisis averted. But it wasn't just me, it was the technology. It was the microwave. *Vorsprung durch Technik.*

The microwave has bestowed better sleep on us all, made our relationships better.

But ten years from now, it may not be like that. The twelve-year-old calls at 6.30. "I won't be home 'til

8.30." "But I've made Lasagne Verde alla Siciliana." "I'll microwave it when I get home." The fourteen-year-old doesn't call but turns up at 10.30 and pops lasagne in the machine. The sixteen-year-old turns up at seven in the morning and has it for breakfast. "Great lasagne, Dad." Yup, great lasagne, but no family meal.

Technologies affect relationships – sometimes for the better, sometimes for the worse, sometimes saving labour and freeing up time for relationships, sometimes reducing the incentive to eat together. The decision to buy a microwave will have an impact on relationships. Naturally, that doesn't mean that you don't buy it because of the potentially negative impact on relationships, though you might not – one friend told me that the best thing that ever happened to her prayer life was not buying a TV – but rather that you recognise and anticipate the consequences. If you buy a TV for your bedroom and you're married, don't be amazed if you see a reduction in the amount of sleep and sex you have.

So Jesus' response to the teacher's question, "What is the most important commandment of all?" not only clarifies God's priorities, it provides a tool for us to consider almost anything we do. After all, the command to "love" is a relational command.

Indeed, as we've seen with the example of the microwave, when we ask how a decision might affect my relationships with God and with people, suddenly it helps us see the benefits and the pitfalls more clearly.

However, the relational lens is not only a means of examining our own behaviour, it is also a diagnostic tool in analysing everything from karaoke to housing policy.

Should we in Britain, for example, have built those sixties concrete tower blocks that came to dominate our inner-city skyscapes? They weren't bad because they were ugly – they aren't. At least not from a distance. They weren't bad because they were an inefficient use of space or funding. Functionally efficient they were – the modernist's dream realised in concrete. They were bad because they failed to preserve or create vibrant, safe communities. They became relational deserts where delinquent jackals prowled and neighbours did not know each other – contexts without community spirit – with graffiti on the walls and needles in the vandalised playgrounds. The design didn't serve to nurture relationships but rather to make them more difficult.

Design affects relationships.

Sometimes positively. Sometimes negatively. If you build housing units, as some builders have done, in which there is no space to put a table for a family to eat round, is it any surprise that family relationships suffer? If, in a country where people live in smaller houses, the church sells off its spacious vicarages in order to release money for other projects, have they perhaps not also just squandered one of the most important assets they had – a house big enough to host those parties, large Bible studies, prayer meetings, bring-and-share lunches that serve to build better relationships in community? It still may be the right thing to do, but introducing a relational dimension highlights what may be lost or gained.

Since almost everything we do, every decision we make affects relationships in some way, what more specific guidelines can we bring to bear to analyse the current health of our relationships and assess the likely impact of decisions we make?

*Shared joy is a double joy:
shared sorrow is half a sorrow*

Swedish Proverb

*Eating meals together as a family is a
predictor of educational attainment.*

Keep Time for Children[1]

*Concern for relationships is a vital part
of sustainable development—whether
economic, educational or social—and
must feature in political debate
and decision-making.*

Clive Mather,
President and CEO Shell Canada

*Leaders choose teams
but eating together builds them.*[2]

Ferndale Proverb

Chapter 4

GETTING RELATIONAL THINKING TO WORK

OR
THE POWER OF CHOCOLATE

Not so long, long ago in a company not particularly far, far away, a young scientist called Anita pondered the utter absence of relationships in her workplace. Every day, the "team" would come in, suit up in white and scurry like moles into the single-person labs that the purity of their research required. Occasionally, one of them would scuttle out, take a domestic beaker and mix boiling H2O with a naturally occurring brown organic compound, rich in caffeine and antioxidant flavonoids. Then they would scamper silently back to their lab to imbibe the solution alone. No one talked to each other, no one shared ideas about the research they were all doing, no one really had much fun. So the young scientist decided to do an experiment and announced that the following Friday, she would make coffee for everyone at 10.30 and she would bring chocolate biscuits.

And so it was that on Friday at 10.30, all the scientists scampered out of their single-unit labs, lured by chocolate, like mice by cheese, into Anita's benevolent conversational trap. Over coffee and biscuits they talked about life, about the news, about their research, about the coming weekend. And week by week, calorie by calorie, the "team" became more of a team.

When Anita left the company, no one made coffee on Friday mornings and no one brought in chocolate biscuits. Six months later, the situation was so dire that the company hired a management consultancy to do team-building exercises. It cost a fortune. And all they needed was a packet of chocolate biscuits and someone willing to make a pot of coffee.

Anita saw the problem and she identified its cause: people had no reason or permission to meet together. So she created a reason to meet together and gave everyone the kind of direct contact with one another that is essential for good relationships and better work.

Relational thinking may sound somewhat theoretical, but it is often worked out in very simple ways. Still, the first step is to see what is inhibiting the relationship.

Over the last twenty years, the Jubilee Centre, the Cambridge think tank founded by Michael Schluter, has identified five factors that tend to predict or lead to what they call "relational proximity", or closeness. These factors have also been used to analyse a wide range of types of relationships, not only in families but in companies, in public institutions like prisons and the tax office, with tangible, measurable results. As you read them, you might want to consider how your own relationships – institutional and personal – might be enhanced by these guidelines.

I. DIRECTNESS OF CONTACT: MAXIMISE IT

A kiss on the cheek is better than an "X" at the bottom of a letter, the touch of someone's skin is better than a photo, and a face-to-face conversation is almost always richer than a teleconference. We are made of flesh, not silicon – at least most of most of us is. We are created to relish physical presence, to grow most through direct contact. That's what Anita's chocolate biscuits facilitated – direct contact.

Direct contact almost invariably builds deeper understanding than physical absence. Being there is better than sending emails or virtual communication and usually more effective. This is, of course, common sense. However, such common sense was much challenged in the 1990s and the early years of this century as businesses sought to increase efficiency and reduce travel costs and carbon emissions through increased use of technology. However, true communication is more than the transfer of information. "Being there" facilitates touch – important even in the simplest of transactions – and increases the accuracy and richness of the communication. Indeed, in any oral communication, words can make up as little as 7 percent of the message.[3] The rest is voice tone, gesture, body language. There are, after all, lots of ways to say the words "Did you buy tickets for the theatre?" Including with an utterly disbelieving, disdainful raising of the right eyebrow.

Directness of contact has proved so vital that a number of businesses have brought back tea ladies, their trolleys and their tinkling bells – not out of nostalgia for ye goode olde days. Quite the opposite. Many businesses found that their employees, like Anita's colleagues, had become bound up in their technologies, sitting in their cubicles, emailing people in the next cubicle and rarely bothering to even try to communicate face-to-face. The result was not only a less satisfying work experience but lower productivity.

However, when the tea lady's bell tinkles, no one has to ask for whom it tinkles ... People have permission to join the queue and chat for a while, sometimes about football, *Desperate Housewives* or the new man in accounts, but often about those little "by the way" bits of business that are actually more efficiently and easily taken care of directly. In either case, overall levels of communication and camaraderie improve. And so does productivity.

Similarly, in today's office environment, there is almost never a convenient time to spend half an hour eating a sandwich with someone over lunch, even if half an hour is actually only fifteen minutes and it's in a cubicle – dining *al desko*. Besides, as Gordon Gecko famously intoned in the film *Wall Street*, "Lunch is for wimps."[4] Nevertheless, over time, spending fifteen minutes munching a sandwich with a colleague once a week can be hugely effective in enhancing efficiency.

Directness of contact is also a useful criterion in the family. How much direct contact do you have? How often do you eat together? And how many of you are there for the whole meal? As author Pat Spurgin put it, "The cement of all relationships is talk." And it's tough to talk to someone who isn't there or who's watching the TV, as around a third of British people prefer to eat their meals."[5]

So how can you create the kind of dynamics that will build deeper relationship? How can you create opportunities for "directness of contact"?

In one case, the dishwasher broke. The parents had two teenage children. What should they do?

Have it repaired?

Buy a new one?

They decided to do neither.

Instead, the parents took turns washing the dishes with one of their teenagers.

After all, you are more likely to have an accidental deeply meaningful conversation about life, the universe and the perfect boy/girlfriend with your teenager in the relaxed atmosphere of doing the dishes than in response to the question: "Why don't we go into the living room and have a nice chat?" Interestingly, when the teenagers left home for university, the parents promptly went out and bought a new dishwasher.

The memorable moments that bring people together – the great laughs, the shared disasters, the wonderful sense of being understood – can as easily occur in a traffic jam, during a frenetic project or doing the shopping as in a chi-chi restaurant or savouring a hazelnut soufflé with the candlelight glinting in your eyes.

Creativity and discernment are required. Buying a 2,000-piece jigsaw puzzle to finish over the Christmas holidays strikes me as an advanced form of psychological torture. However, for some people, it's a stimulating, cooperative venture that can be nibbled at, left, returned to on your own or in pairs or threes or fours or sevens and can create precisely the kind of ease that allows conversation to meander from the incidental to the intimate and back again without pressure.

The key issue here is awareness. On the one hand, as we said earlier, we may have a lot of direct contact but may not have found a way to do anything with it – like a parent who spends hours ferrying a child around in the car to various activities and, in the flurry of it all, doesn't see the opportunity it presents. Interestingly, when people go to business meetings, they plan what they want to get out of the meeting. What would happen if, as we made our way home, we took a couple of minutes to consider how best to make the most of the coming family meal?

On the other hand, we may simply need to create opportunities for direct contact. That's why some couples arrange date nights and others schedule sex – unspontaneous, even unromantic as that may initially seem. Still, it has the advantage of valuing that aspect of their lives that is so easily buffeted aside by the gusts and squalls of everyday living. And at least you know when to take a shower. Or get a headache.

Directness of contact also contains a component of intensity. How emotionally and mentally "there" are we when we're physically there? This idea of "intensity" explains why some encounters have an impact out of all proportion to the amount of time spent – someone hugging you when you really need a hug, for example. Even a stranger. As happened to me once at a speaking engagement when, for reasons that had nothing with the response to my talk, I felt raw, wounded, empty of the resources to face what I thought was waiting for me. Then a woman, clearly enthused by what she'd heard, came up to me and asked if she could give me a hug. She really didn't need to ask. Similarly, it is not just the singer James Blunt who has had the experience of seeing "her face, across a crowded space," not knowing what to do but sensing that they "shared a moment that will last forever".[6]

Directness of contact doesn't guarantee intimacy, but without it you're very unlikely to experience it.

2. CONTINUITY OF CONTACT: TREASURE IT

I grew up in a little suburb called Northwood on the edge of Greater London. From the age of about ten, my mum would send me down to the shops with money, a list and a pencil to write down what I'd paid. I'd go and see Mr Allen, the grocer, who was always happy and always knocked a few pennies off the bill, and then on to Mr Worbouys, who looked like a proper butcher, burly and red-jowled and a little bit fearsome. They'd know my name and ask after my mum, and then I'd pop into Carey's to buy eight nails and put it on Mr Greene's account. But now, thirty years later, I have to get in the car, drive four miles, get stuck in the ring-road traffic round Watford to have the deep joy of going into some hardware hypermarket called Seek & Queue on the off chance that they might actually have what I want, to be greeted by no one at all, and then scurry round the aisles like a blindfolded toddler in Hampton Court maze, chasing the always receding figure of a salesperson I have never met and who not only doesn't know my name but doesn't know my mother's name either. Only to discover that they don't have what I'm looking for, but that Nails R US might – which requires another trip round the ring road. And this, I'm told, is progress.

Nevertheless, in the decade or so after leaving home, I'd go back into town and there'd still be people I knew and who would know me and ask after my mum. There was something warming about that continuity of relationship, about there being people you knew and who knew you, even if not necessarily very well, people you felt a definite affection for. But all those shops have closed now, and when I go to the supermarket, the people on the checkout seem to be different every time and they don't know my name and no one ever takes a few pennies off the bill. Computers don't work that way. Something's been lost.

How arid so many of our sorties into the world now seem. No wonder so many people shop on the Web.

Of course, auld acquaintance is not necessarily best acquaintance, but there's something about old friends – they know just how many times you floated into a room to announce that you'd met the perfect partner, they know how many diets you've been on, they know you were never ever a size twelve, they remember that you were once a great dancer, that you have always had a way with young people, that you lost your first child. You don't have to start all over. Or, in our high mobility, high turnover culture, over and over again. Indeed, as a nation, most of us have fewer friends than our counterparts fifty years ago, and we are much more likely to live more than half an hour's drive away from relatives. And much less likely to work in the same company for ten years, never mind our whole lives.

Continuity builds trust, not only in the family but in the workplace and in the church. Continuity of presence within a particular community allows a number of relationships to flourish at different levels. Obviously, we can't be best friends with everyone, but after a while just the fact that we have been around people in our work or in our town or our club for years develops affection and a sense of belonging and trust.

Continuity of relationship matters, so when we are thinking about moving jobs or houses or towns or countries, we need to ask ourselves how it will affect our relationships. And whether the relational sacrifice is actually worth it.

3. COMMONALITY OF PURPOSE: CLARIFY IT

It was the end of the season. Not my season, but the end of my son's Saturday morning football coaching sessions. The coaches had decided that there would be a fathers-against-fathers match and that they would join in. The coaches were for the most part under thirty. And the fathers for the most part were over forty. And to the naked eye, and I include myself, we looked somewhat beyond full-fledged matches involving anyone who can run a mile in under a quarter of a day. But, we were told, it would be twenty-five minutes. So we went for it, most of us without boots or anything resembling proper soccer kit.

Of course, this being England, the fathers who had been faithfully watching their progeny from the sidelines had hardly talked to each other for the whole season. Still, as we eyed each other somewhat nervously, there were already the flickerings of an embryonic respect, somewhat suppressed by the more urgent hope that we would a) survive without the need for an ambulance and a defibrillator and b) not play so badly that our sons put themselves up for adoption.

Still, it felt like backs-to-the-wall, not-really-ready-for-the-battle, ill-equipped, not-a-pair-of-Nike-90s-between-us, but, hey, needs must – Dunkirk spirit and all that sort of stuff.

So we huffed and we puffed and the wind blew the ball around. Twenty-five minutes passed. Slowly. But they passed. The whistle blew. Grimaces turned to grins, chests expanded, relief abounded. Then we discovered it was twenty-five minutes *each way*. Huffs turned to wheezes that sounded like chalk across a blackboard, and puffs turned to red-cheeked, doubled-over, hands-on-knees, hurricane-force panting.

But we survived. And as we left the field, something had changed in all our relationships. It wasn't just that that round ball of a man, scarcely five-foot-six and surely overweight, had the agility of a squirrel and the shot-stopping capacity of a truck, it was more elemental than that. We'd all got through this unexpected challenge, and we'd had a good game. So there was a warmth as we left the field, eye contact and genuine smiles as we shook hands. We'd connected. If we'd started the season with the fathers' match, we would have had a lot more fun watching from the sidelines.

Shared activity, shared purpose, shared experience bind people together.

And when we share goals, it often diminishes personality tensions or helps to resolve them more quickly when they occur. Wars, for example, tend to focus even ethnically diverse nations. Many people who lived through World War II still reminisce about the positive sense of community they experienced. And as President Barack Obama has pointed out, this is one of the reasons that the US politicians who emerged in the postwar years were so much more respectful to one another than the bulk of their successors: they'd fought a war together, they'd put their lives on the line for a cause greater than pretty much any issue they were likely to disagree on in Congress.

The impact of commonality of purpose on relationships is also clear in family, community, church and working life. People motivated by a clear common cause tend to be more productive and satisfied. A family that's involved in the "family" project together and recognises their shared commitment to helping one another flourish is ever so much stronger than a gaggle of individuals loosely joined by genes, shared facilities and occasional meals.

Interestingly, as it relates to the workplace, an alarming number of workers don't know what's expected of them and how or why what they do fits in with the institution's goals. Employees may have a sense that they are there to make a profit for the shareholders but, beyond that, what is the company's purpose?

Indeed, as Collins and Porras demonstrated in their book *Built to Last*, the most consistently profitable companies are not those that focus on profit but on some higher goal.[7] So people need to know how their work contributes to the realisation of that higher mission and to be convinced that the mission is indeed worthwhile. One man is chiselling stone, another man is building a cathedral; one woman is making furniture for science labs, another woman is facilitating the safe pursuit of knowledge for the benefit of humankind; one teacher is teaching kids enough mathematics to get a C, another is helping them grow into fully rounded adults with enough self-respect, enough self-confidence and enough self-knowledge to find a role that contributes positively to humankind.

Interestingly, the same applies in the church, where an alarming number of people have very little sense of what the church is there to do other than to carry on doing what it is already doing. Indeed, whilst it is certainly true that one of the best things you can do for a lonely person is to give them something to do, particularly if it involves others, people actually need to know why they're doing it. Are they serving coffee because people need a drink after seventy-five minutes in a service? Not a bad reason, by the way. Or are they seeking to facilitate conversations that deepen friendships and open up new ways to encourage one another in the high calling that God has given each one? Is there any sense of how these essential, though mundane, tasks serve the great task of bringing God's love to the world?

Community without purpose is a dead and deadening thing. But shared purpose builds community and releases creativity.

4. MULTIPLEXITY: FOSTER IT

Jane was my boss, a tall, elegant, understated English lady, just thirty and not yet married – I've had worse assignments. She had been in advertising since she was eighteen and was just getting into her stride. She ended up as vice chairman and one of the most adored and respected people in the agency. I ended up adoring her too. She seemed utterly at home in the metropolitan world in which she moved – cabs and clients and nice restaurants and a penchant for twinkly things that her salary did not yet give her an opportunity to celebrate. Then she invited me down to her home in the country. It was a little cottage with a smallish garden split between English flowers and a vegetable plot that yielded all kinds of good things and was the beginning of my love for purple sprouting. And there she was, more at home than in the urban scene, in Wellington boots, not Prada, with thick gardening gloves to protect her parabolic nails, making interesting meals from home-grown produce and taking me on long walks through the Wiltshire countryside. It was in a way a revelation, consistent, of course, with what I knew of her as a person who appreciated the good things in life but making me realise that the range of the good things she appreciated was so much wider than I could have guessed – and so much wider than mine. And so our friendship grew.

People who see one another in more than one kind of context – a multiplexity of contexts – are more likely to develop and maintain deeper relationships. This makes intuitive sense. If I only see a person in one context, in which they are required to play a particular role, wear particular types of clothes, and, in general, confine their conversation to a relatively narrow range of topics, how

well will I know them? But if I see them in another context – at a football match, screaming out their lungs in
a vein-bursting apoplectic crimson rage at the arrantly
unjust and galactic incompetence of an official – I get
a different picture. Hence the value of office parties,
off-site team-building exercises and excursions to the
pub. Or indeed family days. It's quite helpful for people
to see where spouses/friends/parents work – even if it's
only a desk wedged between banks of filing cabinets
behind a pillar in a windowless corridor – as my first
office was. (My colleagues called it "the hutch" – not
that I'm bitter, the carrots were large.) And it's quite
helpful to meet some of the people they work with
and they to meet you: you're real and that secretary
he raves about is sixty-two, not twenty-one. Or she's
twenty-six, and on a scale of 1 to 10, she's an 11. Now
you know what he faces every day.

"Time for a new job, darling."

Or a new secretary.

This insight also explains the potential value of some
corporate entertaining. When I used to work in advertising, I rarely spent my entertainment budget, despite
being encouraged to do so. Sadly, there was a little bit
of the legalist in me that somehow regarded corporate
entertaining as a form of bribery – stick with us and

you'll get to go to the US Open. But at its best, corporate entertaining is a legitimate attempt to develop trust by widening the scope of the relationship. Many high-level decisions may well still be made on the golf course, and this may not be because senior executives are swept off their feet by the sight of a well-manicured green but rather that on a golf course there are usually not lots of other people around. In that context, senior executives can say what they think, express a level of doubt or lack of understanding that might be difficult in a meeting with ten subordinates hanging on their every syllable and expecting them to be incisive and decisive. The same applies at any level: the better the relationship, the more likely trust and understanding will grow.

Multiplexity can be applied to families and church contexts too. Has the married couple's relationship been narrowed down to domestic duties and parental responsibilities? How are other important and enjoyable activities preserved? In what kinds of contexts do parents relate to their children? Is it too narrowly confined for parents to get to know their children or for children to get to know their parents? Indeed, there is some evidence that parents with daughters are slightly more likely to divorce than parents with sons. And the reason, given that it tends to be fathers who are required to leave the family home, is that men, though they may love daughters as much as sons, actually feel more bound to sons because they have a wider natural repertoire of leisure activities to share. The old adage was that the family that prays together stays together, but might it also be true that the family that plays together stays together?

Or, looking at a church context, does the church offer her people a range of ways to relate, not simply in what might be called overtly "ecclesiastical" activities – prayer, Bible study, worship – but in activities that allow people to express other aspects of their humanity – informal suppers, book clubs, sports teams, clean-up-the-neighbourhood days, and even, heaven forbid, quiz nights where you discover that that shy, somewhat retiring individual actually knows more about life, the universe and everything than Wikipaedia and has such a comprehensive knowledge of music that they can tell you the name of the bass player on every top-ten album since the invention of the wind-up gramophone. Of course, it may not be immediately obvious how such a discovery might further the cause of the gospel. Still, it's no trivial thing to appreciate other people's enthusiasms and accomplishments. And besides, might they not be the perfect person to introduce to that music-obsessed work colleague that you've been meaning to have round for supper?

5. PARITY OF POWER: PROTECT IT

Her name was Philippa-Jo Dobson, which sounds rather grand, but most people called her Jo. That being her name, I used it too. Still, I preferred to hail her as Jo-Jo, punching the syllables out in exuberant, somewhat infantile delight. Sometimes I'd call her PJD as if our operation were a sleek, stainless steel, impersonal paragon of cool corporate efficiency. Jo was our receptionist and events manager and conference manager and probably a whole host of other things that I, as executive director even of a small team, was only dimly aware of. That was her job. And she was good at it. My job was rather different. I'm meant to be good at speaking in public, at connecting theology and ordinary life in a way that is both authentic and feels possible. On my team, I have people with a high level of theological acumen, and they help me do things better. We also have experienced speakers and seminar leaders who can not only tell me that something worked well, or didn't work at all, but also spot why.

Anyway, after one evening engagement, I receive some feedback from Philippa-Jo through another "junior" member of staff about what I'd said and how I'd said it. And it was probably the most helpful piece of feedback I'd received in three years. She simply said, "When Mark speaks, even on a familiar topic, but out of what God is doing in his life at the time, it is so much more powerful."

Jo is not a trained theologian, though she is very astute theologically. Jo is not an experienced public speaker, though she leads worship in her church. But she, like the rest of the team, is committed to us all doing what we do as well as we can under God. She could have supposed that she shouldn't say anything, and so could the person who passed it on. Still, in healthy organisations, like healthy families, everyone should have parity of power – an equal right to express their opinion, make a contribution, have their voice heard, and feel that they can ask the CEO not to call them PJD or Jo-Jo, if it turns out to be a source of niggling irritation rather than soaring delight.

It is, after all, the powerful who tend to assign people the nicknames that are used in public. And this applies as much to adults as children. Indeed, the principle of parity would mean that "Big Nose" – a nickname that has been applied to me for reasons which only an elephant or toucan might dispute – gets to choose whether he wants to continue to be called "Big Nose" and whether that is as appropriate in a board meeting as it is over a meal with old friends.

Of course, people are not equal in their skills or knowledge and so should not have an equal "say" in how things are run. I don't know a great deal about running conferences. I don't know as much about technology as the director of operations at LICC (The London Institute

GETTING RELATIONAL THINKING TO WORK

for Contemporary Christianity). Actually, I don't know as much about technology as my fourteen-year-old son. Or my twelve-year-old daughter. Actually ... I don't know much about technology. But as a user, it's important for me to have my say. Similarly, a welder may not know as much as the company finance director about structuring loans, but he or she should certainly have some opportunity to comment on the consequences for their company. All people are created in the image of God and are worthy of respect and dignity and entitled to a voice.

One person's superior competency in one area should not lead to treating people as inferior beings nor to the assumption that those less competent in a particular area do not have something to contribute that may turn out to be vital.

Take the recent global financial crisis. We had devised a system so complex that it was almost impossible for a non-expert to comment without being dismissed as ignorant. But what we have learned is that 99.98 percent of the world's financial experts were wrong, that they were not as smart as they or indeed we hoped they were. We also learned that those financially unsophisticated people who had qualms about the ethics of an economy where so much money was being made on money rather than by making products or offering services were right to be concerned. And we learned that we hadn't found a way to listen to those voices. On a smaller scale, company suggestion boxes are a small but significant manifestation of a belief in the parity of power.

The apostle Paul illustrates the concept of parity by using the metaphor of a body to describe the church. Every part is vital, though clearly each part has a different function. The finger may not be as good as a foot at rifling a soccer ball twenty-five yards into the top right-hand corner of the net, but a finger can point out that an opposition player is lurking unmarked on the edge of the box. Similarly, as Jesus pointed out, adults have something to learn from the faith of children, even if he wouldn't have advocated putting a six-year-old in charge of the local synagogue.

This concept of parity has clear implications in a whole host of areas – from labour relations to family. As union leader Tom Jones put it, "There has never been a strike about pay – only about pay differentials."[8] People usually don't strike because they want more money but rather because they feel that they are not getting a fair share of the money available. Indeed, over the last thirty years, the pay of top-level executives no longer bears any logical relationship to the pay of those who work for them. In a context where the pay differentials between CEOs and junior employees have risen so rapidly, and in some cases, to a factor of over 300 to 1,[9] it's easy to see why many workers have come to feel resentful, particularly when big salaries are not dependent on spectacular performance and when huge bonuses can be paid to people who have actually bankrupted the companies they work for.

For many people, such differentials seem to flout a basic principle of proportionality – are the highfliers really making that big a contribution? And are they really sharing the risk? Similarly, a big company has considerable power to abuse its suppliers by squeezing them on price to the point of unprofitability. The small company clearly doesn't have parity of economic power, but should they not have the right to make a fair profit too?

And this applies in the family. Who has a voice? One of the most countercultural aspects of the Jewish Passover service is the moment when the youngest male child present asks the Four Questions to discover why this night is different from all other nights. The practice dignifies the simplest question. It communicates that we all need to know why we do things, whatever our status. It reminds us that we are all meant to be included, not as mere functions but as people created in the image of God who are part of this unfolding drama in time and eternity.

Later we'll look at how the five criteria might apply to relationship with God, but for the moment, consider your relationships at home, at work, in your local community, club or church. How would you describe them? And what might you do to improve the directness, continuity, multiplexity, priority of purpose and parity of the ones that are important to you? (Go to *www.licc.org. uk/relationships* for some exercises to help you do just that.)

In daily life, what we think, what we say, what we feel, what we buy, how we dress affects our relationships – with God and with our neighbour – so considering our behaviour in the light of its consequences on relationships is vital. At 3.42 in the morning. And 3.42 in the afternoon.

So yes, we might agree that relationships are really important. But still, we might ask, why does Jesus say that nurturing healthy relationships is the most important thing in life?

*Your are a person only because
of other people.*

Zulu Proverb

*Science concluded that isolation was
as significant to mortality rates as smoking,
high blood pressure, high cholesterol,
obesity, and lack of physical exercise.
In fact, isolation is more likely to
kill you than smoking.*[1]

Chapter 5

TWO'S COMPANY, THREE'S A PARTY

OR
A TALE IN TWO PARTS

A TALE IN TWO PARTS – PART I

Not so long ago, I found myself on the platform at Bond Street tube station. I don't mean to imply by the phrase "I found myself" that I had no consciousness of how I got there or that, just a nanosecond before, I had actually been on the *Starship Enterprise* and had been beamed down by the accommodating Scotty. Or indeed that, like Philip, one of Jesus' disciples, I had moments before been on the road from Jerusalem to Gaza, talking to an Ethiopian eunuch reading Isaiah, and then was suddenly taken up by the Spirit of the Lord and deposited in Azotus, probably around forty miles away. No, the first thing I mean to say by the phrase "I found myself" is that I was there, as indeed

I am wont to be four or five days a week. The second thing I mean to say about the phrase "I found myself" needs to wait for its moment.

Anyway, there I am standing on the platform with a colleague and listening to the London Transport employee in her blue and orange uniform telling us about the next train. And I'm thinking, "She's got a good voice and she's using it well." The announcement is clear, beautifully enunciated without officiousness, pretension or embarrassment. I'm impressed. As the train starts to trundle in, I walk up to her and say, "You've got a great voice." In case you're worried for me, I have, I think, reached an age where such actions are unlikely to be viewed as the tactics of a predator.

Anyway, the smile that beams across her face is marginally wider than the train that I scuttle onto. For some reason, I feel absolutely great. Much better, as it happens, than the time I gave a train driver I'd just met a note of consolation and a wooden cross after he'd told me about his disappointment at not being promoted. No, I feel absolutely great – something akin to pure joy.

All of which may seem to have very little to do with the question: Why does Jesus put such emphasis on the quality of our relationships? And the simple answer is that he just can't help it. Anymore than Tigger can help being bouncy, Eeyore morose, or Peter Rabbit mischievous.

I grew up in a Celtic-Pict, Scottish, Russo-Polish, Jewish kind of family. And a very kissy, huggy, touchy kind of family it was. Essentially, my mother had two rules:

1. If it moves, kiss it.
2. If it's still moving, feed it.

She really couldn't help it. Never mind that we were living in the more restrained, cooler environs of middle-class suburban southern England, never mind that most of my teenage friends didn't come from a Jewish background, never mind a Celtic-Pict, Scottish, Russo-Polish background … there was no escape. She couldn't help it.

Indeed, the key to really successful recruitment is not to look for people who can do what you want done but rather to find people who can't help doing what you want done. David Beckham would have played football even if he'd been born in the 1930s, was being paid fifty rupees a week and couldn't afford a swanky Gillette razor, never mind a sleek Italian suit. Similarly, if Pavarotti had been marooned on a desert island, he would probably have sung arias to the birds.

Similarly, Jesus can't stop loving and can't stop being concerned about the quality of our loving. For three main reasons:

I. GOD IS LOVE.

And Jesus is God. And his nature is to love. He just can't help it. That's also why the greatest commandment is "Love God, love your neighbour", because it's the command that most closely reflects God's nature and most accurately clarifies his priorities.

2. GOD LOVES PEOPLE.

And wants the best for them.

And the best and the most satisfying and significant thing a person can do with their life is to love – to know and enjoy the King of the universe intimately and to give their life to loving him and the people he gives them to love.

Interestingly, research has shown that good relationships are actually good for your health. People of faith, that is people with a relationship with God, live longer, recover from illness more quickly and report better sex lives. Similarly, married people live longer and are happier than the single, the divorced or the widowed and are much less likely to suffer from depression. This, of course, may not be primarily to do with being married but with being involved in nurturing, committed relationships. And that, of course, is just as possible for single people, as the longevity of nuns and monks who live in community suggests. Though, of course,

I'm not suggesting that the only paths to long life and happiness are to be found through marriage or monasticism – apparently blueberries and fish oil also help. No, simply put, good relationships are good for you.

Another reason why Jesus is so concerned about the quality of our loving, of our relationships, is that:

3. GOD IS A RELATIONAL BEING IN HIMSELF.
He is three – Father, Son and Holy Spirit – in one.

Precisely how three persons can be one is, of course, a mystery, but it is the picture the Bible paints. God is not some remote *Star Wars* – like force in an infinite, impersonal universe, but personal and relational in himself. Indeed, God the Father does nothing on his own but always in relationship with the Son and the Spirit. Yes, the Father creates the universe, but he does so with and by the Son, through the agency of the Spirit.

> In the beginning was the Word, and the Word was with God, and the Word was God. He was with God in the beginning. Through him all things were made; without him nothing was made that has been made.
>
> John 1:1 – 3

Jesus, the Word, is clearly seen as co-Creator, whilst in

Genesis we read that the "Spirit of God was hovering over the waters" (Genesis 1:2).

In his earthly life, Jesus maintains this three-way relationship. At his baptism, God the Father literally speaks out his approval, and God the Holy Spirit comes on him. This Trinitarian initiation is followed by a life that Jesus leads in a dynamic relationship with God the Father. He says, for example, that he only does what he sees his Father doing and only speaks the words he has been given by the Father (John 12:50).

Furthermore, it's not just that God is a relational being, it is that he wants to involve human beings in the relationships of the divine community. God may not "need" our company, but he certainly desires it. So in John 17, Jesus prays for his disciples, present and future:

> That all of them may be one, Father, just as you are in me and I am in you. May they also be in us so that the world may believe that you have sent me (v. 21).

The Trinity is not an exclusion zone. Access is not only possible, it is fervently desired.

In sum, the Christian understanding is that God is in himself/themselves relational.

Indeed, this is one of the great distinctives of Christianity. Christianity is essentially a relationship with a person. Not a system, not a set of rules to be followed, but a person to know. This is the heart of the matter. God wants to know us and be known by us.

Could there be a greater affirmation of human worth than the startling truth that the King of the universe, the Creator-Redeemer of all, actually wants a relationship with us? You are not just a cluster of amino acids among 6 billion clusters of amino acids on this golf ball of a planet, spinning in an almost infinite universe; you are loved by the triune God who wants a relationship with you in time and eternity.

And he's made that possible through Jesus.

Relationship is so important to God because he is intrinsically relational. And he wants us not only to relate to him but has designed us for relationship with other human beings. Indeed, the first negative note that sounds in the Bible relates to the absence of human relationship. In the biblical account of creation, God pronounces everything "good" until he says: "It is not good for the man to be alone. I will make a helper suitable for him" (Genesis 2:18). Of course, at one level Adam is not alone. God is there. And God is not just there in an ethereal sense, he is there in a physical way that Adam can recognise. In Genesis 2 God brings the animals and the birds to Adam to see what he would call them, and in chapter 3 God is described as "walking in the garden in the cool of the day" (v. 8).

However, despite God's actual presence, it is "not good for the man to be alone". To flourish, human beings require not only an environment that provides oxygen, food, drink, opportunity for purposeful activity, for responsibility, for creativity and for relationship with God – all of which God has already lavishly provided – people need relationship with other human beings.

God may be "enough", but human beings are not designed for that to be the case in their everyday living on earth. Human beings are designed to need others, designed for relationship with others, designed to love and be loved, designed to be interdependent, not independent.

This understanding of who we are as human beings goes against the whole force of Western culture since Descartes said: "I think, therefore I am."[2] This statement not only summarised his view that the primary characteristic that distinguished humans from animals was our mental capacity to reason, it also ushered in the age of the individual, the illusion that people can achieve fulfillment on their own and that independence is a high and noble goal.

The Bible stands foursquare against this. We love, therefore we are. *Amamus ergo sumus.*

We need others if we are to be fully ourselves. Indeed, when God says that he will make a "helper suitable" for Adam, he does not mean someone to carry Adam's bags or tidy his desk, he means a person without whom Adam simply, absolutely cannot do the job that he's been given to do. And it's a big job: nothing less than the stewardship of the planet – the release of its potential and the care of its resources. Elsewhere in the Bible the word for "helper" is applied only to God and almost exclusively in situations where decisive intervention is required – this is about a helper who rescues you from disaster, not an assistant who puts the sugar in your coffee.

So, our goal as humans is not a glorious independence but the high adventure of creating a better world through right relationships. We simply cannot achieve what we are designed for without other people.

The isolated human is an aberration.

This is not simply that we cannot fulfill the tasks given

to us without others – hunt mammoths, build schools, play lacrosse – it is that we cannot become who God intends us to be without relating to other human beings purposefully and positively. We cannot love. The person who does not love is less than a person is meant to be. That's why Jesus commands us to love. Selfless love is the only path to fulfillment. Isolation is not good. Community is good. Indeed, when the apostle Paul describes the transformational impact that the Spirit of God is intended to have on people's characters and actions, he begins his list with "love".

A TALE IN TWO PARTS – PART 2

We are most like God and our true selves when we love.

And that's perhaps why I felt such joy on the platform at the Bond Street tube station. I had in a modest way, for a moment at least, done something unselfish, injected a smidgen of appreciative relationship into a situation normally bereft of it. I had acted in the way I should act: honestly, purely and just a little bit courageously. And there was nothing in it for me – except the joy of giving joy. Of course, it was a tiny thing, and I know that loving strangers is sometimes easier than loving a difficult colleague, and I know that taking ten seconds to tell someone they're doing a good job is a lot easier than giving up an evening to listen to a grieving mother or writing a cheque to help some refugees, but still, finding myself on the platform at Bond Street, I also found myself, for a moment, the more Christlike self I'd like to be more often.

And I experienced something akin to pure joy.

The heart is the saviour of the world.
Heads do not save. Genius, brains,
brilliancy, strength, natural gifts do not
save. The gospel flows through hearts....
It is the heart which surrenders the life
to love and fidelity.[1]

E.M. Bounds

But as I rav'd and grew more fierce and wilde
At every worde,
Methought I heard one calling, Child!
And I replied, My Lord.

George Herbert, "The Collar"

Chapter 6

THE LONG GOOD LOVE STORY

OR
MAKING THE DESERT BLOOM

Afterwards it all looked rather different.

At the time, I'm twenty-three, sitting in my room in one of the best universities in the world, nursing my bad back and contemplating my impending entrance into the wondrous world of work. And Steve Wexler, a fellow student, asks me if I'd like to pray a prayer that places my life in Jesus' hands.

At the time, it seemed to be about Steve and me and God. But over the years, it becomes clearer. There was Big John and Owen and Graham and Hazel and a brace of Christophers who all talked to me about Jesus for years, even though I was usually just looking for loopholes in their thinking. There was the university missioner I "beat" in an argument, only years later to realize I'd lost; there were those Christian neighbours to the right of us and to the left of us; there was the principal of the local Bible college who was one of my father's patients; there was that chaplain at school who told me and another seventeen-year-old boy what he really thought about sex before marriage and, risk of all risks, informed us that he was a virgin and that he expected that his wedding night would probably be the most embarrassing night of his life. There was the drama teacher who cast me as Jesus and the following year as God – it was all downhill after that. There was the senior chaplain who let me lead a chapel service even though I was Jewish; there was the Scripture teacher at primary school who encouraged us to learn all those verses by heart ... Only God knows how many more people, how many beautifully crafted coincidences, how many gentle proddings of his Spirit beckoned me on ...

At twenty-three, perhaps I'd have said that God had been pursuing me for four years. Fourteen years later, perhaps I'd have said that he'd been after me all my life. Now I'd say that the tokens of his love are more numerous than I could list, even if I were aware of half of them ... it's a long love story.

Of course, it's more appealing to try to obey a God

who loves you than a God who is indifferent, but that still doesn't make loving easy. Imagine, for example, that your boss asks you to take on a really difficult project. What do you expect from that boss?

Clear direction, appropriate resources, training, ongoing encouragement. And probably a pay rise at the end of it all.

A life of loving God and loving others is a really difficult project.

It's probably more satisfying than the alternatives, but it's still a really difficult project – loving people in the good times and the bad times, for richer and for poorer, in sickness and in health, loving people when it isn't returned, loving people when you really don't like them, loving people in the way that they are open to being loved even if that is so much less than you'd like to give.

One of the ways that God provides direction, training and ongoing encouragement to love is through what he has revealed about himself and his priorities in the Bible. Indeed, the moment you begin to read the Bible through the lens of Jesus' commands, it opens up fresh new vistas. What does this story tell me about how to love God? What does this tell me about the character of the God who commands me to love him? What does this tell me about how to love others? What examples do I find to follow? What examples to avoid?

Essentially, the Bible is the story of how the right relationships God yearns for are created, how they are broken, and how he then takes the initiative to help people live with the consequences of their actions and rebuild their relationship with him and with others.

THE BLAME GAME

So, after Adam and Eve turn away from God, the consequences hit their relationships first. They go into hiding. They hide from God when he next comes walking in the garden, and they hide their nakedness from one another since they are no longer comfortable being naked in front of each other. But God comes looking for them and asks Adam "why?" Adam points the finger not only at the woman but at God himself: "The woman you put here with me – she gave me some fruit from the tree, and I ate it" (Genesis 3:12). It's the first recorded instance of the blame culture.

Humans have been blaming other people, and God, ever since. Indeed, the further a society moves away from God, the more likely it is to become finger-waggingly legalistic and self-righteously litigious. If in doubt, sue. Even if you happen to be a thief who has broken into someone else's house at night and tripped and hurt yourself, sue ... you might win. And in the UK, the thief in question did.

Whilst Adam and Eve's betrayal shatters the perfection of their relationships with God and with each other, God's yearning for restored relationship with human beings is the heartbeat behind all that follows. His determined love flows outwards to people and through people to other people and through people into organisations and structures and systems.

With Abraham, God initiates a relationship of promise, making a covenant, a contract with him, as a king might with a vassal, or an employer with an employee. God promises Abraham and his descendants good things – a land, nationhood, blessing and the high honour of becoming a source of blessing to all people on earth. Abraham is not just a receiver of God's love but a channel for it, a pipeline to all humanity and all creation. In return, Abraham doesn't have to do anything. He doesn't have to pay tribute, or taxes, or meet quarterly performance targets; he just has to trust God and behave accordingly. God's loving blessings are entirely free.

Certainly, later, when God directs Moses to lead the people out of Egypt, away from grinding slavery, mass infanticide and poverty, he sets out a whole range of commands. These commands, however, are not like the labours of Hercules: impossible tasks designed to thwart their happiness and bring about their death. God doesn't rescue his people out of Egypt to torture them, like some cat that has plucked a mouse from a running stream in order to torment and kill it. On the contrary, he's promised them a land flowing with milk and honey – life in abundance.

Indeed, God's commands are given for people's good. I command my children to pick up the frying pan by the handle – not by the side – not because I want to prevent them from discovering the wondrous joys of holding it by the side, but because I don't want them to burn their fingers. So it is with God's commands: they are for our benefit. And they are all relational, designed to help people create a society that will foster human flourishing, that will allow his love to flow outwards.

Indeed, Jesus clarifies how love is the shaping spirit behind all the other commandments. Just a few days before he was executed, Jesus finds himself in direct confrontation with the religious leaders of his time in the temple in Jerusalem (Matthew 22:35 – 40). They try to trap him by asking him which is the greatest commandment of all. He not only tells them – love God, love your neighbour – but clarifies that all the teaching in the Jewish Bible stems from those two commandments. This then is the lens through which to look at all the other commandments.

So if we take one of the Ten Commandments, like "You shall not steal", and look at it through the lens of the Great Commandment, we can see that God's primary concern is not about property but about how theft reflects a deep disrespect for another person. Theft denies relationship; theft breaks relationships. The law, then, is not primarily concerned with the preservation of property but with the development and preservation of good relationships between people. Similarly, take one of the other 613 commands that the rabbis had identified, "Do not hold back the wages of a hired labourer overnight." A hired labourer would not have had any savings, so he needs his wages straight away so he can feed himself and his dependents. It's not loving to let a man and his family go hungry because you can't be bothered to pay him for work already done. Still, how many bosses actually fail to pay their employees on time? And how many companies deliberately pay their suppliers so late that the suppliers go out of business?

Similarly, the command not to reap to the very edges of a field or gather the gleanings of your harvest comes out of love. It expresses God's concern that the poor should be able to find food, that we recognise our duty of care to those who don't have enough. It also reflects God's concern that the rich should not be so concerned to nail down every last penny of income that they forget either the source of their income or their duty to be generous to their fellow human beings.

So God says, "You shall not murder" (Exodus 20:13) because people are valuable to God and he knows we won't enjoy living in the fear and anxiety and chaos that mar a murderous culture – even if *you* survive. He says, "You shall not give false testimony" (v. 16) because a culture where lies are told and justice breaks down oppresses people. He says, "You shall not commit adultery" (v. 14) because adultery shatters relationships. The Ten Commandments are not the ten life-deniers but the ten life-enhancers.

Obeying God's commands is therefore, like honesty, the best policy. Even if in the short term it may not always seem so. Sometimes we obey through clenched teeth, every subatomic particle in our being screaming to go in a different direction: I would really, really like to take that bribe; I would really, really like to sleep with that person ... But will it bring me good, will it bring others good, will it make our community better, or will it be just one more drop of poison in the well that will bring sickness and pain to us all?

Ultimately, obedience to God should not be the grudging, fearful subservience of an oppressed slave, but the willing, willed, trusting response of a daughter to a wise and benevolent father.

THE ROAD TO LIBERATION

Jesus puts it this way:

> If you love me you will obey what I command.... Whoever has my commandments and obeys them, he is the one who loves me.
>
> John 14:15, 21

The commands of God are good news for people, a "delight", as Psalm 119:35 puts it. They help to foster intimate relationship with him. And they direct us to the kind of behaviours that will serve to create, nurture and protect healthy, productive, caring, joyous communities, to generate the social capital that is in increasingly short supply.

Interestingly, the Bible calls this kind of behaviour "holiness" (see Leviticus 19).

Holiness is often perceived to be an entirely ethereal, otherworldly quality – a smiling, beatific, quasi-elfin aura, a nonchalance in the face of pressure or catastrophe. However, whilst holiness may spring from character, it expresses itself in how we live our daily lives, as indeed the Holiness Code in the book of Leviticus makes clear (chapters 17 – 26). Ultimately, holiness is love flowing out in thought, word and deed. In corporate social responsibility. In a fair return for tea growers in Assam and seamstresses in Thailand. In befriending the person that no one else talks to in the office. In getting that job or that homework or that manuscript completed on time so that others are not inconvenienced.

Holiness is an expression of love.

Just as the waters of the River Nile break its banks every spring and flow into the bordering fields, so God's love is always seeking to flow out into the world. People may build barriers to it, or channels for it, but either way his love still seeks to reach the withered soul and the parched heart and the arid nation. Indeed, God's concern for the other is intended to flow out beyond the needs of any immediate community, out to the alien, the foreigner, the people who are not part of our gang, our gang, our gang.

That's why Jesus' injunction to love God and love our neighbour is not only the best idea in the world but the best idea *for* the world. Only the kind of love that flows across borders has the capacity to overcome the rivalries of our riven world.

We, like Abraham, are created to be channels of his love to others. Treating people well is important to God not just because God is seeking to preserve the harmony and good relationship of existing communities but because all human beings are created in the image of God. All are therefore infinitely valuable to him and worthy of love and care. Indeed, in Jesus' parable of the good Samaritan, it is not the Jewish priest or the Jewish expert in the law who shows compassion for the traveller mugged on the road to Jericho, it is the Samaritan, a man from a community that the Jews of the time despised. Who qualifies as my "neighbour" is not determined by tribal affiliation, by socioeconomic status, by race, gender, colour or creed, but by what my heart is like.

The key question, then, is not who qualifies to be my neighbour, but whether I am "neighbourly", whether I have a heart of compassion for those in need – whether that's the homeless person outside the supermarket, the secretary with a headache or a Massalit man in Darfur. Jesus doesn't ask us to consider whether a person in need qualifies for our concern, but rather to consider the state of our hearts. He doesn't ask us to calculate what percentage of our income we give away, but to consider what our neighbour's needs are.

Of course, it's possible to devote oneself to a life of

praising God but ignoring one's neighbours. It's possible to turn up on a Sunday in a church, sing your heart out and run a profitable business all week that exploits your workers and ravages the planet. It is theoretically and practically possible to pray fervently to the God who said, "Love your [wife] ... as Christ loved the church" (Ephesians 5:25), and beat your wife. But that is certainly not God's desire. Biblically, you simply cannot love God with all your heart without at least seeking to love your neighbour. Because *he* does. Love him, love his kids.

Indeed, sometimes a misdirected desire to please God can sidetrack us from his priorities. So, for example, Jesus sharply criticises a group of zealous Pharisees for tithing mint and rue but not looking after the poor (Luke 11:41 – 42).

The Pharisees were so concerned, and probably sincerely so, to "love" God, to obey God's laws, that they entirely lost sight of his priorities – the poor are more important to God than a tiny pile of herbs.

People before parsley.

Similarly, Jesus cautions those who bring their sacrifices to God:

Therefore, if you are offering your gift at the altar and there remember that your brother has something against you, leave your gift there in front of the altar. First go and be reconciled to your brother; then come and offer your gift.

Matthew 5:23 – 24

Make it right with people first.

Of course, ensuring we have perfectly harmonious relationships with other people is not a prerequisite for a flourishing relationship with God. After all, we can't force people to forgive us. Still, we can make a determined attempt to bring about the kind of relational reconciliation that God desires, even if sometimes people won't or just can't forgive us. Nevertheless, when they do, it makes you feel like dancing.

FORGIVEN AND FORGIVING

Inevitably, other people hurt us – sometimes in terrible, terrible ways. But if we don't deal with the reality of the hurt we feel, with the anger, with the desire for revenge, the sense of injustice … if we suppress all those feelings and don't find a way to forgive, then the wound festers and its sulphuric pus bursts out in spiteful words, in petty machinations, perhaps in violence. As writer Neil Anderson pointed out, when we are wronged, one thing is clear: we will live with the consequences of what was done or said, whether we like it or not. So the choice we have is whether to live in "the bondage of bitterness" or "the freedom of forgiveness".[2]

Forgiveness does not mean sweeping the issue under the carpet but rather dealing with the mess together. When we don't forgive, we build a wall against love, and it is we who are trapped behind it. That's why Jesus puts such an emphasis on forgiveness. Indeed, in the prayer he taught his disciples, "Our father who art in heaven", only one of the requests carries a condition: "Forgive us our trespasses as we forgive those who trespass against us." In other words, if we want God to forgive us for the ways in which we have rebelled against him, rejected his ways, taken him for granted, then we need to forgive others.

And isn't it such a liberation, such a relief when there are no landmines buried in the space between you and another person?

NEIGHBOURHOOD WATCH IN THE GLOBAL VILLAGE
This inclusive understanding of "neighbour love" at the personal level obviously also has profound implications for the way nations interact in a global economy in which we not only produce more than enough food to feed every human on the planet but also have the transport capacity to deliver it.

It is not loving to pay a Nicaraguan or Kenyan or Colombian coffee grower so little for their beans that they cannot afford to feed their children or even roast, grind and drink the very coffee they pick.

It is not loving to pay so little to the Malay who makes our clothes – in conditions we wouldn't wish on a rat – that they can hardly afford to clothe their own children.

God is the Creator and God of the whole world, so our concern for right relationships must be global in scope. Individually, we may not, in the short term at least, be able to affect global trade policies, but we can write to our politicians and lobby our supermarkets and buy fair trade bananas – even if that means that we may have to make do with four instead of five.

So holiness becomes real when holiness is expressed both through devotion to God and through loving action towards our fellow human beings.

Jesus clarifies the startling scope of the command to love in the Sermon on the Mount, calling on those who follow him to love their enemies and to bless those who persecute them. Initially, this seems absurd. How are we to love our enemies? But this is what God does. God's love flows out to all people. He sent his Son for all people, even the enemies who defy him, as we all have done. And so we are to imitate God in loving our enemy even if their behaviour cannot be condoned or go unpunished.

Furthermore, this is the only way to break the spiral of vengeful violence that ravages so many nations and communities. Nelson Mandela, for example, brought peace to South Africa after the long years of apartheid by choosing to love and forgive the people who had imprisoned and persecuted him and his people. If he had sought revenge, it would have triggered a bloodbath.

Forgiveness is an offer of love to another, an invitation to renewed relationship, a setting aside of the past for the sake of a better shared future. Can we really imagine a good future for our planet or indeed for our own nations without it?

GOOD RELATIONSHIPS AND GOVERNMENT POLICY

The Bible then reveals the long good history of God's determined love, a love with the goal not just of individual intimacy but of global good order and generosity.

Jesus' commands make "good relationships" the goal of any social system, the goal of the whole world order, where "good" is defined by the kind of love for God and others he demonstrates. Good, then, not in the sense of affability, but in the sense that the system of relationships is "good news" for people, regardless of national identity or economic or social status. Government policy should seek to create conditions in which good relationships can flourish, in which populations are drawn together in common goals that benefit all, not just the powerful.

The Christian cannot sit in splendid isolation and simply look after themselves and their immediate family. As Merry said to the Ents, the great trees in The Lord of the Rings, when they had decided not to join the war against the Dark Lord: "But you are part of this world."[3] The Christian is called to love, to seek the welfare of the company they work for, the town they live in, the society they are a part of and the planet they share. Indeed, this is precisely what God tells the Israelites who had been forcibly deported to pagan Babylon:

> Seek the peace and prosperity of the city to which I have carried you into exile.
>
> Jeremiah 29:7

The pursuit of holiness is then the pursuit of intentionally selfless loving relationships and of intimacy with God. And the commandments that God gives are not hurdles that people need to jump in order to be in relationship with him, but rather loving beacons that show how that relationship is to be lived out day by day in the cultural context of their own time. They show people how to love God. If you want to love me, God says, love your neighbour, your coworker, your boss, your enemy.

If you want to love me, love my kids. All of them.

And here are some ways to do it.

Shared joy is a double joy;
shared sorrow is half a sorrow.

Swedish Proverb

All real life is meeting.

J. H. Oldham

Q: What is the No. 1 casualty of a busy life?
A: "Intimacy with God."

— Ken Costa

Love bade me welcome …

George Herbert, "Love (III)"

Chapter 7

INTIMACY AND THE DIVINE

OR
TALES OF FISH AND LIVER

If we are perhaps clearer about what loving our neighbour might mean, what might loving God look like? Or, more specifically, what might a dynamic relationship with God be like?

Imagine you're a fisherman, a professional, and you've been out on the lake all night, throwing out the nets, hauling them in – empty. Throwing out the nets, hauling them in – empty again. You're wet. And by four in the morning, even in the spring in Israel, you're cold through. On the shore 100 yards away, a man calls out, inquiring if you've caught anything. You tell him. And he tells you to throw your nets over the right side of the boat. It's dark, it's 100 yards away and he couldn't possibly see a shoal of fish from there that you can't see from where you are standing in the boat, but you throw out the nets anyway – and you can't haul them in because they're too full. You make your way to shore.

The night has ended better than you could have imagined, but you're still wet and cold and no doubt hungry. But there are fish to haul in and count and distribute to the crew, the boats to beach, the nets to hang and the journey home to complete before you'll get anything warm in your belly ...

But there on the beach you can see a wood fire glowing orange and yellow in the dark, and wispy spirals of smoke and steam rising into the cold night air. And you can hear the sizzle of fish oil as it drips into the fire and the occasional sharp crackle as a flame leaps up and singes the fish's skin ... and the man says, "Come and have breakfast."

You weren't expecting him. He was dead, after all. But he's there anyway. Jesus, risen from the dead, with a myriad, myriad things he could be doing, a whole universe of places he could choose to manifest his bodily presence, but there he is, King of the universe, making breakfast on the beach for his friends after a long night's labour on the lake. Love is thoughtful. Love is practical. Love is hot grilled fish and bread, right there. And then.

And now?

We were both students. What they call in the UK "mature" students, defined purely in terms of age, it should be noted. Over twenty-five. And recently married and, though certainly not poor, not exactly flush with cash. At the time, a local rather high-class store used to deliver a rather high-class selection of food that had reached its sell-by date to the college we were studying at. So, at the end of the day, the students who lived off campus, far, far away from the delights of college dining, would hover like seagulls behind a trawler, waiting for the day's catch. It was exam time and we were, I think, weary with revision. As I was about to leave home to join the circling seagulls, my wife said, "I fancy some liver." This, I hasten to add, is not a phrase often heard in Britain – liver not being a particularly popular dish. In fact, in all my time as a circling seagull, I couldn't remember a time when liver had arrived. It was as if she had asked for Galapagos Turtle. Still, I took off and the day's delivery arrived. There was steak and chicken and wonderful bread and fruit. The seagulls swooped and dived with all the elegance and politesse of a pack of jackals and came up clutching their trophies in their triumphant talons. "Anyone want this?" came a voice. "What is it?" "Liver." No one swooped, no one dived, no talon stretched out to grasp the package of burgundy flesh from the emptying crates. Except mine. Liver. Very fine calf liver and more than enough for two, though not quite enough for three.

It was the only day that the high-class store ever delivered liver.

A coincidence? Perhaps. But a gift, it seemed to us, from God. A gift, not even in response to a prayer, just in response to a preference. Love is thoughtful, love is practical. Love is hot grilled fish for a tired fisherman and succulent liver for a weary student, right there. Then and now.

Love takes risks, asks for a rendezvous that you may reject, makes an offer that you may refuse, proffers a gift you may return. Love never compels.

Love sends flowers, writes a note, buys tickets for music you adore – even if it puts them to sleep. Love puts a chocolate on the desk, the kind of chocolate you like – Swiss, smooth, milky with whole hazelnuts. Love dashes out to get you a sandwich when you don't have time – hummus on dark rye bread with sliced tomatoes and fresh-milled black pepper. Love cuts out the article you might have missed, puts out the trash, prays that your friend will call when you're down ...

Love bids you welcome ... invites ... offers.

Love listens.

Love banishes the fear of being known and rejected. Love rebukes because love wants the best for you. Love corrects you to raise you up, not to put you down; to liberate, not to imprison; to free, not to suppress the real you, the possible you, the fruitful you.

Love does not pacify, love empowers. Love coaxes the bud into bloom.

Love sits with you in pain and exclusion, gives you time when your mind no longer knows what time is or who you are. Love makes sure your hair is well cut even when only the sick are there to see it. Love hides you under the table from Nazis, as Corrie ten Boom hid a Jew; love volunteers to take your place in Auschwitz's starvation chamber, as Father Maximilian Kolbe did; love does not exact revenge against you, but walks the long road to reconciliation as Nelson Mandela did; love lays down their very life for you – as Jesus, son of Joseph, did.

Love will wait to give, but love's waiting is active ... it never stops yearning for union.

Love wants your love.

> All night long on my bed
> I looked for the one my heart loves;
> I looked for him but did not find him.
> I will get up now and go about the city,
> through its streets and squares;
> I will search for the one my heart loves.
>
> Song of Songs 3:1 – 2

Love takes the initiative, makes an offer you can refuse …

God is love.

And so it is that God the Father, out of his desire for relationship, for union with us, sends his willing Son to die on the cross.

THE GREAT COMMANDMENT IN ACTION

On the cross we glimpse the depth of what loving God and loving neighbour might have meant to Jesus. For Jesus, loving God with all his mind, heart and strength meant agreeing to go through terrible pain to do God's will. Loving his neighbour as himself meant going through terrible pain so that all humankind might have a relationship with God the Father, as Jesus does.

Indeed, Jesus' loving initiative not only opens the way

to restoring our relationship with him to the level of the uninhibited intimacy that was experienced in Eden, it creates an even more amazing possibility – a relationship of the intimacy that Jesus describes in John 17:

> My prayer is not for them alone. I pray also for those who will believe in me through their message, that all of them may be one, Father, just as you are in me and I am in you. May they also be in us so that the world may believe that you have sent me. I have given them the glory that you gave me, that they may be one as we are one: I in them and you in me (vv. 20 – 23).

This does not cease with mortal life but continues into immortal life where the prayer finds its ultimate fulfillment.

From relational rupture in the garden of Eden to relational rapture for eternity.

God's love is forever love.

Nevertheless, this relationship is not for its own sake. Jesus is, after all, sending his disciples into the world to change it. Unity with God is the prerequisite for effective engagement in the world and the essential resource for it.

Still, we're created not only with a desire to make a difference but with a yearning for a love that will last forever.

That's why so many love songs sing of eternal love. Dido won't ever raise a "White Flag"[1] on her love, the Dixie Chicks promise to "never, never give you up".[2] Yes, the intimacy of a satisfying marriage is a joy indeed and celebrated in the Bible with love poetry that beautifully melds the romantic and the sexual:

> Let my lover come into his garden
> and taste its choice fruits.
>
> Song of Songs 4:16

But even that cannot meet the need for the kind of forever love humans are created for.

No, as Jesus' prayer clarifies, those who follow him are in the Father as he is in the Father and will in eternity know the perfection of intimacy. However, such intimacy doesn't mean we lose our identity. We don't drown in God's love but soar on its wings.

INTIMACY AND INDIVIDUALITY

When we die, we will not evanesce into nonconscious nothingness within the Godhead as in Hinduism nor undergo a Pullmanesque molecular merging with nature. Rather, our unique God-created identity will be preserved. Just as the identity of Jesus, God the Son, remains distinct from his Father's identity even though they are intimately and inextricably connected, so we as human beings retain our individuality. Indeed, in the new heaven and the new earth, even though we will have new bodies, we will be recognisable as the same person we were.

The purpose of Jesus' self-giving on the cross was therefore not only so that the penalty for human rebellion would be paid off, nor that people would be ransomed out of the dominion of darkness – though Jesus did pay that penalty and people are rescued from living under Satan's malicious rule. No, the ultimate purpose of Jesus' self-sacrifice was so that we might enjoy an uninhibited, eternal, transformative, satisfying, intimate relationship with the triune God. Tyndale, the first translator of the Bible into English, coined the word "atonement", "at-one-ment", to capture this idea. Through Jesus' sacrifice we are "at-oned" with him.

Indeed, though there are few things sweeter than being forgiven, the yearning of the human heart is not primarily to be told that we are forgiven but for the restored relationship that forgiveness creates.

We want more than legal absolution, or a clean record,

or an official pardon; we yearn for the ease, the openness that was there before – the sweetness and relief of embrace now that the hurt and anger and guilt have been swept away. Of course, in human marriage, this may express itself in sex, and some say that "make-up sex" is the best kind, but even in sex the abiding memory may not be of the particular intensity of the physical pleasure but of the look of love on the beloved's face as it is given. We yearn for restored union.

This idea of closeness was inherent in the early sacrificial system that God instituted. Indeed, one of the key words for sacrifice used in the book of Leviticus is *karav*. And the root meaning of *karav* is "close, near". So to bring an offering to the altar is in Hebrew *yakriv karav* ... "to bring close a closer". In the New Testament, the theme of closeness is expanded. We read that after Jesus died on the cross, the veil that used to cover the entrance to the Holy of Holies in the temple, the place that only one chosen priest could enter and only on the Day of Atonement, was torn in two from top to bottom by God.

OPEN ACCESS

The implication of this is clear: the way to God is open at all times for all people. The writer to the Hebrews makes the same point. Because of what Jesus has done we can "approach the throne of grace with confidence, so that we may receive mercy and find grace to help us in our time of need" (Hebrews 4:16).

Still, the closeness that Jesus envisages is not primarily about physical proximity, like getting close to a famous person. Nor is it primarily about physical touch, like the physical touch that John the disciple would have experienced when leaning on Jesus' chest at the Last Supper. The closeness that Jesus envisages is not in "space" – he hasn't simply moved into the neighbourhood or the spare room or sat down at the kitchen table – no, the closeness Jesus envisages is in our very "being". Jesus has moved into our inner being by his Spirit. Indeed, on the eve of his death, he tells his disciples that it is better for them that he goes away physically:

> But I tell you the truth: It is for your good that I am going away. Unless I go away, the Counsellor will not come to you; but if I go, I will send him to you.
>
> John 16:7

This Counsellor, as John makes clear, is the Holy Spirit, the third person of the Trinity, who will dwell inside the disciples and will teach, guide and strengthen them. This divine presence, the inner assurance of God's love and constancy, is their source of peace, their shalom – whatever the world throws at them. So God's desired relationship with us is not mere closeness, he is not merely "there", not just "with" us, like an accompanying angel, he is "within" us.

And so it is that we do not need to visit a building to pray to God or set aside special times to talk to him. There is always access. That's why the apostle Paul can encourage Christians to "pray constantly".

Prayer is not dial-up, but broadband.

It isn't a call to a secluded life in a monastery, a convent, or a lonely hut on some bleak and wuthering height, but a reminder that God is in us by his Spirit, that we have open access to communing with him at all times – in offices and factories, kitchens and schoolrooms, in sickness and bombardment, and in the valley of the shadow of death.

So, for example, one Western business person returning from serving the people in a third world slum, said, "I have never experienced such a sense of the presence of God in my life, as I did when I was in that place." And he said it in an adult Sunday school class in a rich suburb. That, of course, is not to say that other Western business people don't experience God's presence in their ordinary everyday work in the affluent West. One man put it this way to me: "When I work at my company, I feel God's pleasure."

And so we can see here how the five relational factors we looked at earlier – directness, continuity, multiplexity, parity and commonality of purpose – might apply not only to our relationships with people but with God.

THE GOD WHO IS THERE

First, we need directness of contact. We don't just want to read about God or hear stories of what he's been up to in other countries or in other people's lives; we yearn to hear from him ourselves, to know his presence ourselves. That requires time set aside for him – as a married couple might set aside time just for each other even though they have nineteen children, five dogs and an aardvark. However, it also, and sometimes more challengingly, requires a greater consciousness of God in our everyday tasks and encounters. Just as the warmth and attention of a host can transform a simple meal of beans on toast into something that feels as lavish as a feast and you as honoured as royalty, so inviting God into our ordinary, everyday lives opens the way for us to see how he might touch and transform the ordinary with the fragrance of beyond.

THE GOD WHO DOESN'T LEAVE

Second, our relationship with God is enhanced over time – with continuity. The longer we're with him and conscious of him being with us, the deeper our trust and delight can grow.

THE GOD INVOLVED IN ALL

Third, our relationship with God is enriched through multiplexity. Through knowing him and seeing him at work in a variety of different contexts and situations, we grow in love of who he is. When he answers prayer for a difficult client meeting (he did), when he restores a lost, very old, literally irreplaceable iron key in response to a child's heartfelt prayer (he did), when his presence is palpable in an Alzheimer sufferer's moment of clarity as a son comes to say "good-bye" (it was) – through such experiences our love and appreciation for God grows.

THE GOD WITH AN OPEN EAR

Fourth, there is "parity of power", but of a particular kind. Of course, no human being is equal to God in any area of competence or power, and yet every human being is valued. Indeed, we see in God's relationships with people that he wants to hear from us, that we have a voice, that Abraham can "negotiate" with God over the destruction of Sodom, that the psalmist can cry out in protest at God's apparent indifference, that Jesus, perfect in obedience to his Father, can ask if there is another way other than the torture of the cross. Furthermore, whilst God could accomplish all that he wishes to accomplish on his own, he chooses to do a great deal of it in cooperation with human beings. We matter in his purposes.

THE GOD OF ADVENTURE

Fifth, the disciples of Christ share a commonality of purpose with God. He has invited us to join with him in changing the world, in caring for the sick, in changing world trade agreements so that the poor are fed and the enslaved liberated, and in modelling ways of living that put people before things, time before money, love before logos, generosity before rights, Christ the Son of God before King Konsummon, son of Mammon.

The Christian, every Christian, is called to be yeast, leaven, an agent of transformation in God's mission of transforming and reconciling and restoring the whole universe. This is the great adventure God calls people to be part of, and the result is that the every day is tinged with the eternal, the routine with the fragrance of forever, the chore with the possibility of being a conduit of love and a channel of his eternal grace.

Indeed, the word "grace" in the New Testament is used in two quite distinct ways. First, it means "undeserved favour" and is used to describe the reality that those who come into relationship with Christ, and therefore enjoy all the benefits of being his children, do not do so through any merit of their own or because of anything that they have done. You can't buy your way into heaven or get into heaven because of wondrous acts of charity, extraordinary beauty or good citizenship. It is a free gift of God – undeserved by anyone.

Second, grace is used to describe God's "empowering presence". So it is that in every single one of his letters, Paul addresses Christians with the words "Grace and peace to you". Since they are all already believers, what Paul is praying for is God's empowering presence with and within them, the grace that enables them to do what God wants them to do, to be who he is calling them to be – whatever the circumstances. Again, this is essentially a relational promise – I'll be there. In power.

We can know his presence – on occasion, almost tangibly – as we do things he wants done, not simply as we speak and listen. Indeed, this reflects the reality that in human relationships, bonds of closeness are not just forged through verbal communication but through the communion-building impact of shared tasks and activities. Somebody can be "known" deeply through their actions and a lasting bond forged without words. Working on a shared challenge can create a depth of respect and commitment out of all proportion to the verbal intimacy shared.

Indeed, the wonder of the God revealed in the Bible, and known in my experience, is that he loves "me", not only in all my faults, rebellions and weaknesses but in particular ways that make his love real to me – like a lover who knows that their beloved's favourite flower is not a rose, or a lily, or an iris, but a daffodil, which was my aunt's favourite flower.

And so it was with daffodils, not roses or lilies or irises, that my mother adorned my aunt's coffin.

And in no less tender and personal ways does our God know and love us.

*Happiness is
when what you think,
what you say,
and what you do
are in harmony.*

Mahatma Gandhi

*"We love because he
first loved us."*

The apostle Paul

Chapter 8

LOVING WITHOUT GOD?

OR
WHAT THE ATHEIST DISCOVERED

We can't really love God without loving our neighbour, but can we love our neighbour without loving God?

At first glance the answer seems to be "Yes, we can".

Lots of people do it.

Parents love their children, even their wayward ones. Children love their parents – even their violent ones. People of most faiths, and none, extend love to people beyond their immediate community – the poor, the marginalised, the drug addicts, the homeless, the chronically sick, the dying. Again, as we saw in the parable of the good Samaritan, it is a foreigner – who is not, in the eyes of first-century Jews, a real Jew at all – who extends love to the stranger who's been left for dead on the Jerusalem-Jericho road. There is no room for Christian self-righteousness here. There are many loving atheists who love their neighbour in ways that Jesus would rejoice in.

And yet, as Roy Hattersley, former member of parliament and self-avowed atheist, pointed out in *The Guardian*: "We have to accept that most believers are better human beings."[1]

By which he meant that believers simply do much more for the sick, the poor, the disadvantaged – even if they don't share their faith – than atheists. And he has the data to prove it. He goes on to write:

> Civilised people do not believe that drug addiction and male prostitution offend against divine ordinance. But those who do are the men and women most willing to change the fetid bandages, replace the sodden sleeping bags and – probably most difficult of all – argue, without a trace of impatience, that the time has come for some serious medical treatment.

Good works, John Wesley insisted, are no guarantee of a place in heaven. But they are most likely to be performed by people who believe that heaven exists.

The correlation is so clear that it is impossible to doubt that faith and charity go hand in hand.[2]

GOOD NEWS IN BLEAK TIMES

Historically the reason, humanly speaking, that Christianity grew was not just because it was true but because it was good news for people's lives and therefore attractive to believers and not-yet believers.

This is brilliantly demonstrated by Rodney Stark in his highly influential book *The Rise of Christianity*.[3] Without diminishing the essential power and significance of Jesus' message and sacrifice, he points out how the Christian response to social conditions and historic events clearly made it good news for others. In a Roman Empire that practiced infanticide of girls and oppressed women through enforced and highly dangerous abortions, the Christian stance against infanticide and abortion was good news for women.

Similarly, when the Roman Empire was hit by terrible epidemics in AD 165 and 251, overall the pagan population neither looked after those who shared their beliefs nor those who didn't. However, the combination of Christian teaching about heaven and loving your neighbour meant that Christians nursed both sick Christians and sick pagans. Independent of any miraculous intervention, the survival rate was higher among Christians and their pagan friends than amongst those who were not connected to Christians. The gospel was good news for the sick. And all this stemmed from Christian doctrines. Beliefs drove actions and offered a highly benevolent alternative to the prevailing culture.

Stark summarises it:

> Christianity revitalised life in Greco-Roman cities (hugely overcrowded, disease-ridden places for the most part) by providing new norms and new relationships. To cities filled with the homeless and impoverished, Christianity offered charity as well as hope. To cities filled with newcomers and strangers, Christianity offered an immediate basis for attachments. To cities filled with orphans and widows, Christianity provided a new and extended sense of family. To cities torn by ethnic strife, Christianity offered a new basis for social solidarity. And to cities faced with epidemics, fires, and earthquakes, Christianity offered effective nursing services.[4]

Interestingly, the capacity of Christian communities to offer a vibrant, attractive alternative to broad societal problems not only in the ancient world but in the twenty-first century was recently highlighted by Matthew Parris, one of *The Times*' leading commentators and an avowed atheist. His travels in the ravaged continent of Africa led him, surprisingly and controversially, to this conclusion:

> Now a confirmed atheist, I've become convinced of the enormous contribution that Christian evangelism makes in Africa: sharply distinct from the work of secular NGOs, government projects and international aid efforts. These alone will not do. Education and training alone will not do. In Africa Christianity changes people's hearts. It brings a spiritual transformation. The rebirth is real. The change is good....
>
> Those who want Africa to walk tall amid 21st-century global competition must not kid themselves that providing the material means or even the knowhow that accompanies what we call development will make the change. A whole belief system must first be supplanted.[5]

The belief system that Parris describes is the tribal group-think, the rural-traditional mind-set that stunts curiosity and initiative and "feeds into the 'big man' and gangster politics of the African city: the exaggerated respect for a swaggering leader, and the (literal) inability to understand the whole idea of loyal opposition."[6]

Parris has not yet come to the conclusion that Christianity is the best idea in the world, but he's certainly convinced it's the best idea for Africa. It's a start.

What Parris rightly recognizes is that ideas have legs.

They take you in a certain direction. Atheism, for example, leads inevitably to a lower view of humankind than Christianity. Atheists, after all, don't believe that human beings are of infinite worth or that actions in this life have eternal consequences. Of course, that doesn't make all atheists inhumane. Still, it is no accident that the atheistic creeds of Stalin, Hitler, Mao and Pol Pot resulted in the murders of more people in the twentieth century than all the wars of humanity – religious or otherwise – throughout human history.

Indeed, history seems to show that the further a society – whether nominally Christian or not – moves away from an understanding of a loving personal Creator who creates all human beings in his image, the more likely that society is to treat people inhumanely or to create conditions in which people feel more anxious and alienated. And that is precisely the conditions we suffer in the UK, the US and Australia.

Secular thinkers, like, for example, the UK's former Culture Secretary Chris Smith, believe that we can recover our kindness as a society without recourse to the well from which it sprang – the good news of a loving Creator. This is rather like thinking that you will be able to take two showers a day for the next month even though your water has been turned off at the mains. He wants the grapes without the vine.

THE LIMITS OF OUR LOVE

If this decline in national goodwill cannot be reversed without God, might it also be true on a personal level? Do we have the capacity to love our neighbour as we would want? Why is it that, whilst we all know that relationships are so important, we seem to find it so difficult to create the kind of relationships we want? What stops us?

Are we able, without divine help, to love the stranger, the alien, the person so much poorer than us, the person so much richer? Douglas Coupland, not himself a person of Christian faith, put it this way in the mouth of one of his characters in his novel *Life after God*:

My secret is that I need God – that I am sick

and can no longer make it alone. I need God to help me give, because I no longer seem to be capable of giving; to help me to be kind, as I no longer seem capable of kindness; to help me love, as I seem beyond being able to love.[7]

How much space do we have in our hearts for others? Can we love as we would love to love without God?

Christianity would argue that the ultimate answer to that is no.

After all, is it so easy to love as God loves? Is it easy to love selflessly, to set aside our own agendas, to quench the oceanic thirst of our egos? Is it easy to die to the insistent demands of me, myself and I? To genuinely and consistently put others first?

Don't most of us need help to do that?

And how does being in relationship with God help us?

First, human beings are not only designed to love, we are designed to know God's love. When we don't, there will always be an underlying sense of dissatisfaction, of restlessness.

Being loved by God fills the need for him that he has

created. Furthermore, it is the soul-deep knowledge of being totally loved and accepted by the most important person in the universe that liberates us from our debilitating concerns about ourselves. *He* loves me – and frees me to love more and more like him – and helps me by his Spirit.

THE ANTIDOTE TO FEAR

One of the great inhibitors in most people's lives is fear – fear of failure, fear of embarrassment, fear of looking odd, fear of death … Fear paralyses action, crushes initiative, makes us look away rather than look ahead, look down rather than look up. Fear is the enemy. Now we know from psychological research that, overall, children who have been raised by loving parents in a secure, stable environment are more likely to be courageous, more likely to take risks, more likely to swim against the popular tide. Love creates a foundation of security that acts both like a springboard and a parachute. Simultaneously, the experience of being loved launches people into adventures that the fearful would not contemplate and catches them when they otherwise might come down to earth with too great a bump.

But suppose we didn't grow up in such a nurturing environment? Are we doomed to be ruled by fear? And even if we did, does human love remove all fear? Does it on its own satisfy the human yearning for eternity, for the love that will never die? Can it remove the fear of death? Or reassure us that our everyday, ordinary lives are actually significant in the grand scheme of things?

No, ultimately, only the perfect love that we can experience in relationship with God can drive out the fear that prevents us from fully giving ourselves to others. For to truly love another is not to need their love in return to carry on loving. We may desire their love, but if we need it, then our love will be tinged with selfishness or fear that the love we need will not be given. If, on the other hand, I know that I am totally loved by God, I don't "need" anyone else's love to keep loving.

So it is no accident that Jesus links loving God with loving neighbour.

Ultimately, neither can be fulfilled without the other.

LOVING BEYOND OUR MEANS

A while back, a man looked me in the eye and told me that his wife didn't love him, like him, desire him, appreciate him or respect him. That doesn't leave much out.

What kept him from bitterness? What kept him from seeking comfort elsewhere?

What enabled him to carry on, standing by her, trying to love her when nothing came back except rejection? To carry on offering the kiss when the kiss was not returned, when she might turn a cheek but never offer her mouth? What kept bitterness from taking root even if from time to time it tainted his tongue? For him, it was the sense of being loved by God, that he was fundamentally OK. God had lined the walls of the man's heart with the reality of his love, and that worked to repel the thoughts of worthlessness and the impact of rejection.

God's command to love does not come without the resources to fulfill it. We cannot fully love God without his help. And we cannot love our neighbour without being in relationship with the God of love who not only shows us what love should look like but empowers us by his Spirit to love beyond our means.

Biblically, it is only by being in Christ that this is possible. Jesus puts it this way: "I am the vine; you are the branches" (John 15:5).

The branches can produce no fruit unless they are in the vine, cannot love as he would have us love if we are cut off from the source of that love. In one of his letters, John the disciple put it like this: "We love because he first loved us" (1 John 4:19).

And that Jesus-love is demonstrated to others by imitating it in action. Here's John again:

> This is how we know what love is: Jesus Christ laid down his life for us. And we ought to lay down our lives for our brothers [and sisters]. If anyone has material possessions and sees his brother in need but has no pity on him, how can the love of God be in him? Dear children, let us not love with words or tongue but with actions and in truth. This then is how we know that we belong to the truth, and how we set our hearts at rest in his presence.
>
> 1 John 3:16 – 19

This, however, is not just an individual response. Those who follow the triune relational God need to show that his church is indeed a model of purposeful loving relationships and a fountain of unconditional love.

Is the church such a model?

The love of the fellowship of the church was overwhelming ... and I said to myself, "These are people that are godly." Yes, they have faults like everyone else as a church, but I was overwhelmed by the help they gave my wife, bringing food to her. They didn't know her, and that just consolidated the faith I had, and still does to this day.

Quoted in *Journeys and Stories*, by Nick Spencer and Peter Neilson

Chapter 9

THE RELATIONAL COMMUNITY

OR
THE CHALLENGE
TO THE CHURCH

Christianity is a relational way of life. And it is for this reason that the church is so vital.

The church is the representative community of the triune God on earth. Our relationships of humble, purposeful, open, vulnerable love are intended to mirror the loving relationships within the Trinity. Indeed, throughout the Bible we see that, though God does call individuals to love and obey him, his desire is to make a people, to create a community. So he doesn't just create Adam, he creates male and female and calls on them to multiply. Similarly, he calls Abraham in order that through him a people, a community, might grow. Furthermore, when someone becomes a follower of Jesus, is "born again" as Jesus puts it, they are not born again into splendid isolation, not simply changed into an individual who now relates in a different way to God and to the people they encounter along the way.' No, the person who is "born again" is born again into a new community, a new family. Indeed, in the New Testament, the antidote to loneliness is not to find a partner but to find a community.

The church ought to be the best place to be single in.

Yours may not be, but that does not obviate the truth that it is meant to be. And could be. Indeed, maturity in Christ cannot be achieved by an individual on their own ... because it is in the community of God's people that wisdom is found. The church is a body that needs all its parts functioning to be whole. And so it is that the quality of relationships within the church are vital. After all, if Jesus' kind of selfless love doesn't bloom in the people who claim to follow him, maybe he hasn't really provided the resources, the power, to live it.

Well, what is the quality of relationships in the church you know?

Probably quite friendly. But there is a world of difference between friendliness and friendship, between affability and a determined, humble commitment to seek the best for other people. There is a world of difference between being able to talk warmly and amusingly about current affairs and the courageous capacity to be who you are truly, to be open and vulnerable with other people. There is a world of difference between confident, flowing conversations that establish one's credentials and credibility as a successful human being and that vulnerable communication that tentatively stutters towards the admission of sin and weakness and need and pain and therefore paves a path to being truly known and truly accepted.

THE JOY OF GENEROUS LIVING

Similarly, there is a world of difference between communities that meet and greet on a Sunday and communities that serve to foster the kinds of relationships that genuinely support one another during the week – communities that make and deliver meals to couples who've just had a child (as some do), communities that don't just pray when your pipes burst but scramble into action and come round, ready to mop and dry, to replaster and repaint (as some have). People who put their time and talent and treasure where their heart is. People who notice that your smallish car is ten years old, has only two doors and one front seat that doesn't fold forward anymore, that you already have two children, and that your wife is heavily pregnant with your third, who help you buy a replacement (as one couple did for my family). People who, when they discover that your wife has to spend a month in hospital before the birth of your third child, offer to pick up your other two children from school and take them to the hospital to see their mother for a couple of hours before the father gets home – as a member of our church did.

What was in it for them?

The joy of living in God's generous ways.

It is indeed more blessed to give than to receive, though I do love presents, nice notes, small amounts of chocolate, wooden toys, kisses, hugs, surprise visits … When we give we enter into God's generous giving nature. Love gives – expecting nothing in return. And this kind of love is one of the primary ways in which people who don't know Jesus will know that Christians are his disciples – apprentices of this particular master – through our love for one another. As Jesus himself said:

> A new command I give you: Love one another. As I have loved you, so you must love one another. By this all [people] will know that you are my disciples, if you love one another.
>
> John 13:34 – 35

The disciple is therefore not primarily someone who knows the Bible, though they may, or who goes to a church building on a Sunday, though they probably will; a disciple of Jesus is someone who loves those who love Jesus in a practical, intentional way. The way of the disciple is the way of selfless love. And one of the goals of the community of Christ is to help us love in this way. Discipleship is therefore essentially learning to love.

Whilst the church as a whole has a poor image, LICC (London Institute for Contemporary Christianity) research reveals that people's actual experience of the Christians they've met and the Christian communities they have experienced is far more positive. Indeed, the example of open, welcoming, caring communities on people's journey towards becoming followers of Jesus seems, if anything, to have grown in significance in the last twenty years. These communities may or may not have multimedia presentation technologies, cappuccino machines and award-winning décor, but people are often simply stunned by the practical, no-strings-attached love of the "ordinary" people they meet and the ordinary-extraordinary ways in which love is expressed.

The representatives of Jesus are therefore to be characterised by the kind of generosity that eases pain, alleviates hunger, liberates from addictions, sets captives free, sets people on a road, seeks the best for people, and wants them to grow in love for God and in practical, humble love for one another.

This is not easily achieved.

The story goes, a true story I'm told, of a pastor going to another church to hear a friend speak. The sermon was all about the need to forgive each other, the need for forbearance and patience. The pastor went away concerned for his friend but delighted because there was no way that he needed to preach such a sermon in his own church. All was zing and sparkle in his garden. But later in the day, it hit him like a rhino: the reason there was no need to preach a sermon on forgiveness and forbearance and patience in his church was because no one really knew each other well enough to be irritated by them. The relationships were gleamingly superficial. Safe, sanitised and achingly hollow.

Surface harmony may actually be a symptom of poor relationships and the consequence of the absence of any shared purpose challenging enough to create any argument about how it might be achieved or any rebuke to those who block progress.

THE COUNTERCULTURAL COMMUNITY
Furthermore, the kind of community the Bible envisages is one where the barriers that tend to exist between

people of different race, age, socioeconomic and educational categories, and even musical preferences, are broken down. In the Bible, we read that "there is neither Jew nor Greek, slave nor free, male nor female, for you are all one in Christ Jesus" (Galatians 3:28). Historically, of course, the church's record has been mixed. But what is the situation in your community? Is there no male and female, no middle class and working class, no graduate or nongraduate, no white, no black, no Asian, no asylum seeker, no teenager or middle-aged? Have the barriers that our society tends to erect actually been torn down and replaced by a deeper reconciliation and love that transcends such categories? Is there any evidence of love for people not like "us"? Is there any generosity for fellow Christians where we don't live? Like the church in a North London suburb that, despite the heavy demands on its own (deficit) budget, still gives £10,000 a year to support the work of a church in one of the poorest areas in the UK. Or the people giving sacrificially of time and money to help orphans in Romania, refugees in Darfur, trafficked children all round the world.

This love is, however, not exclusively for those within the body of Christ. On the contrary, God loves the whole world, and so his people are called to seek the best for all people. Some churches may indeed be wonderful oases of refreshment and strength, but God's plan is not just to create oases but to make the whole desert bloom.

Still, whatever the image of the church, the reality is that in the UK and indeed in the US, no community does more voluntarily for people beyond their immediate family than Christians through churches in formal and informal ways – through youth work, breakfast clubs, homework clubs, social clubs, mums and toddlers, Saturday clubs for divorced fathers, chaplains in hospitals and prisons, counselling, marriage preparation, drug rehabilitation, work among prostitutes and the homeless, the homebound and the hungry, through feeding programmes, by visiting the sick and elderly ...

This is a reality that, in the UK, both local and national governments are keenly aware of. And though this work is often done very openly in the name of Jesus, it rarely requires any faith commitment to receive it. The Salvation Army, for example, does not ask homeless AIDS-infected drug addicts if they believe in Jesus before providing shelter, food, care and a drug rehabilitation programme.

This is not to say that more might not be done. Indeed, in Western nations where there is so much relational deprivation, the scope for the self-giving involvement of the communities of Christ and for much greater synergy between the church and social services is simply enormous.

In sum, the church is intended to be a community where wisdom for fruitful living is passed on through relationships. And such wisdom for life is certainly something that Western culture is yearning for, which explains the growth of mentoring and coaching and counselling and psychotherapy – people looking for people to help them live wisely.

Overall, in the UK, as the London Institute for Contemporary Christianity's Imagine research has shown, the majority of churches are not yet adept at helping people live well in Christ in the rapidly changing culture we find ourselves in, not good at providing wisdom for the various common challenges of life that people face – choosing a life partner, choosing a job, parenting children, creating a home that is a vibrant context for human flourishing, dealing with aging or sick parents, working not only under time pressure but ethical pressure ...[1]

The church's recent focus has been on making converts rather than actively responding to the example Jesus set as he lived his life on earth and the command he gave as he left it:

Therefore go and make disciples of all nations, baptising them in the name of the Father and of the Son and of the Holy Spirit, and teaching them to obey everything I have commanded you. And surely I am with you always, to the very end of the age.

Matthew 28:19 – 20

A disciple, after all, is not a mere student seeking to acquire information but an active, intentional apprentice seeking life transformation, a person who wants to live their life in the way their master lives life, to be holy as God is holy in every aspect of their lives.

JESUS' RELATIONAL WAY

Interestingly, though Jesus spent much time teaching large crowds, he spent the bulk of his time on his relationships with twelve disciples, relationships that required openness, trust, closeness and accountability, relationships full of challenge and tenderness, incisive character insight and determined encouragement. Do you have any relationships like that in your church?

And are the leaders seeking to create a culture that has the same focus on discipleship as Jesus had? A loving culture that is determined to help people to see how to be holy, how to love God and their neighbour, how to be the kind of community that is a compellingly attractive reflection of the outwardly oriented loving relationships of the triune God in our twenty-first-century context? Increasingly, that is what people are looking for and, much to my encouragement, there are signs that more and more communities are taking up the challenge.

"You must sit down," says Love,
"and taste my meal." So I did sit and eat.

George Herbert, "Love (III)"

Chapter 10

GOT A BETTER IDEA?

OR
GIVE THIS ONE A TRY

Love God, love your neighbour. The best idea in the world?

Well, it may have seemed an absurd claim, an adman's claim, but has anyone in history ever come up with a better idea?

Has anyone in history come up with a better, more compelling piece of advice? Think about how what you do, think and say will affect your relationship with God and with others. Live your life in a way that builds your relationship with God and seeks the best for others. It's a piece of advice that addresses the deepest needs of the human spirit, the need to be released from our self-obsession and to find hope and significance and perfect love in a relationship with an eternal God that knows us intimately, always wants the best for us and will never, ever, not ever leave us or abandon us.

A forever love.

Love God, love your neighbour. An idea that is the litmus test for any other idea.

An idea not just with legs but with wings, an idea on which healthy friendships and healthy families and healthy companies and healthy churches and healthy societies can be built. A piece of advice that has the power to transform the world for the better. Which is why it's not just a recommendation from a consultant but a command from the Maker of the universe. It is, after all, *his* world.

And it's an idea that can be lived and is worth giving one's life to and one's life for. Indeed, as we look at what lies behind this idea, we get a glimpse of who God is – of the relentless, life-giving love God has for his world and for us, the astounding truth of how we can be part of the way he extends his love outwards to the people we meet and work with day by day. And we get a clearer understanding of the one who spoke those words, who walked his talk through the dusty streets of Jerusalem and out to Calvary hill.

Has anyone in the history of the world ever lived out their own advice with such sobering integrity?

Has anyone demonstrated the beauty and cost of that idea so wondrously?

Setting aside the glories and comforts of heaven for the ordinary life of a carpenter and the cruel death of a criminal.

Laying down his own life because he loved his Father so much, laying down his own life because he loved his neighbour so much.

Because he loves us so much.

Loves you. Loves me.

And will always be there. With us.

And has been.

And is.

May it be so for you.

NOTES

CHAPTER 2: THE DISCONNECTED HEART

1. Anna Moore, "Eternal Sunshine," *The Observer* (May 13, 2007).
2. "Girl Guides: Red tape deterring adult volunteers", *The Telegraph* (18 June 2008).
3. "Child Poverty in Perspective: An Overview of Child Well-Being in Rich Countries", Report Card 7 (2007), 2. UNICEF Innocenti Research Centre: *www.unicef-irc.org*.
4. Margaret Maed, http:thinkexist.com
5. UK National Statistics: *www.statistics.gov.uk*.
6. Marcus Buckingham and Curt Coffman, *First, Break All the Rules: What the World's Greatest Managers Do Differently* (New York: Pocket Books, 2005); "Feedback for Real", *Gallup Management Journal* (15 March 2001): *http://gmj.gallup.com/content/811/Feedback-Real.aspx*.
7. A UK survey based on exit polls indicated that 70% of employees who quit their jobs quit because of bad managers.
8. "Average home has more TVs than people", based on research by Nielsen Media Research, *USA Today* (21 September 2006).

CHAPTER 4: GETTING RELATIONAL THINKING TO WORK

1. www.keeptimeforchildren.org.uk.
2. Wisdom from Ferndale, the name of Mark Greene's family home.
3. Albert Mehrabian, *Nonverbal Communication*, 3rd ed. (Piscataway, N.J.: Aldine Transaction, 2007).
4. *Wall Street*, directed by Oliver Stone (Los Angeles: 20th Century Fox, 1987).

5. Sophie Radice, quoted in "Hell Is Eating Together," *The Observer* (8 May 2005).
6. "You're Beautiful," written by James Blunt, Sacha Skarbek and Amanda Ghost (New York: Atlantic Records, 2005).
7. Jim Collins and Jerry I. Porras, *Built to Last: Successful Habits of Visionary Companies* (New York: HarperCollins, 2002).
8. Tom Jones, quoted in Michael Schluter, "Pay Differentials and Relationships", Jubilee Centre: *www.jubilee-centre.org/document.php?id=158&topicID=0* (December 2006); Frederick Guy, "Earnings distribution, corporate governance and CEO pay", *International Review of Applied Economics* 19, no. 1 (2005): 51 – 65.
9. Schluter, "Pay Differentials".

CHAPTER 5: TWO'S COMPANY, THREE'S A PARTY

1. J. S. House, K. R. Landis, D. Umberson, "Social Relationships & Health", *Science* 241, issue 4865 (1988): 540 – 45.
2. René Descartes, *Principles of Philosophy* (1644), part 1, article 7.

CHAPTER 6: THE LONG GOOD LOVE STORY

1. E.M. Bounds, *Power through Prayer* (Chicago: Moody, 1979).
2. Neil T. Anderson, *The Bondage Breaker* (Eugene, Ore.: Harvest House, 1990), 100.
3. *The Lord of the Rings: The Two Towers*, directed by Peter Jackson (Los Angeles: New Line Cinema, 2002).

CHAPTER 7: INTIMACY AND THE DIVINE

1. Dido, "White Flag", BMG (2003).
2. Dixie Chicks, "Lullaby", words and music by Emily Robison, Martie Maguire, Natalie Maines and Dan Wilson, Sony (2006).

CHAPTER 8: LOVING WITHOUT GOD?

1. Roy Hattersley, *The Guardian*, Comment (12 September 2005).
2. Ibid.
3. Rodney Stark, *The Rise of Christianity: How the Obscure, Mar-*

ginal, *Jesus Movement Became the Dominant Religious Force in the Western World in a Few Centuries* (Princeton, N.J.: Princeton University Press, 1996; New York: HarperCollins, 1997).

4. Stark, *Rise of Christianity*, 161.
5. Matthew Parris, "As an atheist, I truly believe Africa needs God", *The Times* (27 December 2008).
6. Ibid.
7. Douglas Coupland, *Life after God* (New York: Simon & Schuster, 1994), 359.

CHAPTER 9: THE RELATIONAL COMMUNITY

1. See Imagine research results at *www.licc.org.uk/imagine*.

TAKING RELATIONAL
LIVING FURTHER

If you're interested in exploring relational living further, then both the London Institute for Contemporary Christianity (LICC) and the Jubilee Centre have websites with resources and articles on a wide range of topics, plus information on key books and links to other relevant websites. The two websites are:

www.licc.org.uk
www.jubilee-centre.org

If you're interested in the application of relational thinking to public policy issues, to business and corporate contexts, to the life of your local church and to a wide range of issues in private life, see the Jubilee Centre website (*www.jubilee-centre.org*) and that of its sister organization, the Relationships Foundation (*www. relationshipsfoundation.org*). In particular, small group Bible study and discussion material on building better relationships in churches and communities as well as a DIY audit called "Building a Relational Church" are available from the Jubilee Centre.

If you're interested in applications to church communities or work groups, or you're looking for exercises, resources or Bible studies that help you work through the issues, then look at both the Imagine Project and Engaging with Work sections of the LICC website and consider subscribing to LICC free biweekly short emails – "Word for the Week" and "Connecting with Culture".

Highly recommended resources include:

The R Option: Building Relationships as a Better Way of Life, Michael Schluter and David Lee (Cambridge: Relationships Foundation, 2003) – a lifestyle book that explores relationships as the key to well-being in both professional and private life.

Jubilee Manifesto: A Framework, Agenda & Strategy for Christian Social Reform, edited by Michael Schluter and John Ashcroft (Downers Grove, Ill.: InterVarsity, 2005) – a detailed study of biblical teaching about major policy areas such as welfare, economics and criminal justice, with a view to understanding what a relational society looks like in practice and how we can go about influencing our society in the light of that agenda.

Imagine How We Can Reach the UK (DVD), Mark Greene, LICC – an inspirational DVD resource exploring how church communities can help people grow in living fruitfully in today's culture, available from *www.licc.org.uk*.

Building Relationships Together, Neil Hudson and Tracy Cotterell – eight Bible studies looking at creating a more enriching and selfless community life, free download from *www.licc.org.uk/imagine*.

The Jubilee Centre exists to equip Christians to shape the structures of society according to biblical principles and to live distinctive lives. This is done through a rolling programme of research and initiatives to communicate the fruits of that research to a wider audience. Subscribe online for free to receive "Cambridge Papers" and "Engage" each quarter. For more information, call, write or email:

Jubilee Centre
Jubilee House
3 Hooper Street
Cambridge
CB1 2NZ
UK
Tel: 01223 566319
Email: *info@jubilee-centre.org*
Web: *www.jubilee-centre.org*

The London Institute for Contemporary Christianity (LICC) exists to envision and resource Christians to make a difference in the world, to apply their faith to the everyday situations and challenges of twenty-first-century life. To receive LICC's free quarterly bulletins, subscribe online or call or write to:

LICC
St Peter's
Vere St
London W1G 0DQ
UK
Tel: 020 – 7399 – 9555
Email: *mail@licc.org.uk*
Web: *www.licc.org.uk*

Share Your Thoughts

With the Author: Your comments will be forwarded to the author when you send them to *zauthor@zondervan.com*.

With Zondervan: Submit your review of this book by writing to *zreview@zondervan.com*.

Free Online Resources at
www.zondervan.com

Zondervan AuthorTracker: Be notified whenever your favorite authors publish new books, go on tour, or post an update about what's happening in their lives.

Daily Bible Verses and Devotions: Enrich your life with daily Bible verses or devotions that help you start every morning focused on God.

Free Email Publications: Sign up for newsletters on fiction, Christian living, church ministry, parenting, and more.

Zondervan Bible Search: Find and compare Bible passages in a variety of translations at www.zondervanbiblesearch.com.

Other Benefits: Register yourself to receive online benefits like coupons and special offers, or to participate in research.